TRANSGRESSIONS: CULTURAL STUDIES AND EDUCATION
Volume 67

TRANSGRESSIONS: CULTURAL STUDIES AND EDUCATION

Cultural studies provides an analytical toolbox for both making sense of educational practice and extending the insights of educational professionals into their labors. In this context *Transgressions: Cultural Studies and Education* provides a collection of books in the domain that specify this assertion. Crafted for an audience of teachers, teacher educators, scholars and students of cultural studies and others interested in cultural studies and pedagogy, the series documents both the possibilities of and the controversies surrounding the intersection of cultural studies and education. The editors and the authors of this series do not assume that the interaction of cultural studies and education devalues other types of knowledge and analytical forms. Rather the intersection of these knowledge disciplines offers a rejuvenating, optimistic, and positive perspective on education and educational institutions. Some might describe its contribution as democratic, emancipatory, and transformative. The editors and authors maintain that cultural studies helps free educators from sterile, monolithic analyses that have for too long undermined efforts to think of educational practices by providing other words, new languages, and fresh metaphors. Operating in an interdisciplinary cosmos, Transgressions: Cultural Studies and Education is dedicated to exploring the ways cultural studies enhances the study and practice of education. With this in mind the series focuses in a non-exclusive way on popular culture as well as other dimensions of cultural studies including social theory, social justice and positionality, cultural dimensions of technological innovation, new media and media literacy, new forms of oppression emerging in an electronic hyperreality, and postcolonial global concerns. With these concerns in mind cultural studies scholars often argue that the realm of popular culture is the most powerful educational force in contemporary culture. Indeed, in the twenty-first century this pedagogical dynamic is sweeping through the entire world. Educators, they believe, must understand these emerging realities in order to gain an important voice in the pedagogical conversation.

Without an understanding of cultural pedagogy's (education that takes place outside of formal schooling) role in the shaping of individual identity–youth identity in particular–the role educators play in the lives of their students will continue to fade. Why do so many of our students feel that life is incomprehensible and devoid of meaning? What does it mean, teachers wonder, when young people are unable to describe their moods, their affective affiliation to the society around them. Meanings provided young people by mainstream institutions often do little to help them deal with their affective complexity, their difficulty negotiating the rift between meaning and affect. School knowledge and educational expectations seem as anachronistic as a ditto machine, not that learning ways of rational thought and making sense of the world are unimportant.

But school knowledge and educational expectations often have little to offer students about making sense of the way they feel, the way their affective lives are shaped. In no way do we argue that analysis of the production of youth in an electronic mediated world demands some "touchy-feely" educational superficiality. What is needed in this context is a rigorous analysis of the interrelationship between pedagogy, popular culture, meaning making, and youth subjectivity. In an era marked by youth depression, violence, and suicide such insights become extremely important, even life saving. Pessimism about the future is the common sense of many contemporary youth with its concomitant feeling that no one can make a difference.

If affective production can be shaped to reflect these perspectives, then it can be reshaped to lay the groundwork for optimism, passionate commitment, and transformative educational and political activity. In these ways cultural studies adds a dimension to the work of education unfilled by any other sub-discipline. This is what Transgressions: Cultural Studies and Education seeks to produce—literature on these issues that makes a difference. It seeks to publish studies that help those who work with young people, those individuals involved in the disciplines that study children and youth, and young people themselves improve their lives in these bizarre times.

Go Where You Belong

Male Teachers as Cultural Workers in the Lives of Children, Families, and Communities

Edited by

Lemuel W. Watson
C. Sheldon Woods
Northern Illinois University, USA

SENSE PUBLISHERS
ROTTERDAM/BOSTON/TAIPEI

A C.I.P. record for this book is available from the Library of Congress.

ISBN: 978-94-6091-404-1 (paperback)
ISBN: 978-94-6091-405-8 (hardback)
ISBN: 978-94-6091-406-5 (e-book)

Published by: Sense Publishers,
P.O. Box 21858,
3001 AW Rotterdam,
The Netherlands
www.sensepublishers.com

Printed on acid-free paper

DEDICATION

This book is dedicated to all of our teachers who work hard on a daily basis to change the lives of our students.

TABLE OF CONTENTS

PREFACE

The purpose of this book is to continue the dialogue about the importance of men in the lives of young children and the teaching profession. This book will also be beneficial for those teachers and administrators who work on a daily basis to enhance the education of children in early childhood and elementary education programs. By sharing their stories, male teachers in this book educate the reader about the challenges they face as men; however, their stories also offer solutions and suggestions as how to work with parents, students, peer teachers, and others in order to maximize student achievement. In fact, the male teachers in this volume are sincere culture workers (Freire, 2005) who strive to make a difference a difference in the lives of children, their families, and their schools. This book will inspire others to encourage more men to enter the profession of teaching, especially early childhood and elementary education. Men who are interested in working with young children will have a first hand glance of the journey of learning, playing, and teaching children and working with their parents on a daily basis through these narratives.

A secondary purpose of this book is to bring a more open and honest discourse about the many ways that men contribute to children's development. Through this dialogue, the reader might reflect on the vast array of diversity that exists within racial groups, gender, and sexual orientation. The book helps to broaden the groups "collective identity" and therefore, helps those who work with male teachers to expand their understanding in order to try new ways of helping. Cultural nuances of the professional field must be addressed from multiple levels in order to make an impact on male teachers' experiences. In addition, how male teachers construct meanings of how to live their lives in a society that restricts their own sense of masculinity will be addressed. This text will also provide a good introduction to issues of cultural persistence and transmission in early childhood and elementary education which hinders the progression of gender integration (Schonpflug, 2009).

In other word, the majority of males are disadvantaged by society's strict cultural/ gender norms, and conformity to these restrictive masculine behaviors that not only increases the level of anxiety about being socially ostracized, but also dictates males' range of social, emotional and academic roles and experiences. For example, most of the contact children have with men in elementary schools is normally limited to the principal, facilities personnel, or physical education teacher; and the main reason cited throughout the literature to enhance the number of male teachers is to be positive role models (Buxton, 2000; Sargent, 2002). Hence, the inability to explore and embrace other possibilities related to men ways of being reduces the opportunities they might have in society, especially as it relates to working with children.

This book is not intended to serve as a cookie cutter for men entering early childhood professions or to minimize the contributions of all of our female teachers. Instead, it might serve as a guide to enlighten the reader of the unlimited possibilities and opportunities that exist if we choose to be bold and to have the courage to challenge the status quo in following our own intuition about our life's work as men;

this is especially true for breaking down the cultural transmission of social/cultural gender roles in our society related to men's exploration of traditional female professions.

Audience

The primary audience for this book is anyone who is interested in children's development and ways to enhance their growth through creating a network to support them. In addition, the secondary audiences for the book are students in under-graduate and graduate programs in teacher education and early childhood professions. Administrators and superintendents who are in charge of creating well balanced environment for learning and development will be greatly interested in the narratives of the authors because they offer detailed information about how they worked with their administrators and school leaders to create better learning environments. Practicing teachers and educators will also find this text to be an important professional development tool due to the fact that all teachers are asked to work together to enhance the students' educational outcomes. In each chapter, authors share details about their trial and errors in order to find workable solutions that benefit their classrooms, schools, and partnerships. Each chapter focuses on the challenges and strategies that men utilized to remain in the classroom and to thrive in their personal and professional choices to stay where they belong – with children. This book is also organized and written so that the lay person could read the narratives and be inspired by the authors of each chapter; hence, creating a social network of individuals who support and encourage men to enter the field.

Scope and Treatment

This book provides a perspective to assist educators and professionals in moving their organizations and agencies toward the ideal of a well-adapted educational environment that celebrates the diversity that males and females bring to the class-room. The male voices in this book represent seasoned and novice teachers who have self-identified as male teachers with a story to tell about their experiences with children, parents, peer teachers, administrators, and communities. Rarely does the literature and research highlight for the reader the concerns of male teachers in their own voices. Minor editing has been done for clarity; however, preserving the individual's voices through their narrative was most important. Yet, what we present in this text are the teachers' concerns so that they might be utilized to develop and guide practice. We will give supporting documentation to the reader to help set the context for basic understanding of the materials presented; however, we do not waver with following the naturalistic approach of informing the reader of issues and concerns primarily through out own contextual lenses and experiences.

This book makes a contribution to the existing literature by bringing the reader to the first person narratives by male teachers. The uniqueness of this book resides in capturing some of the authors' experiences from a novice professional to becoming a seasoned advocate for such issues as directors of programs or professors in universities. All of the authors are forthcoming with how they became involved with children, the rewards and challenges. In fact, this book paints the canvas of individuals' life work and their passion and commitment to fulfilling their purpose in the world; it helps readers to see the possibilities of a career in the field and the unlimited options to contribute to the lives of children, their families, and their community. This book will help the reader to understand and connect to authors in multiple ways as the narratives unfold in each chapter. Although the book is about men in the lives of children, it also teaches readers about their "ways of being" as men, fathers, teachers, and humans. This book is like having a personal coach for the novice teacher and a good friend for the seasoned. This book will also include a "resources" section with helpful hint for teachers and administrators.

The true test of any teacher education program is its ability to change, to respond strongly and positively to the emerging needs of society. In that process of change, it must base its decisions on specific and valid academic outcomes, on a vision of sustained growth and measured improvement in its processes and products, and on effective collaboration with all the active players in the educational enterprise, including local school districts, business and industry, liberal arts faculty, and other colleges and universities involved in the same enterprise.

REFERENCES

Buxton, M. (2000). The African American teacher: The missing link. *Black Collegian, 30*(2), 116–121.

Freire, P. (2005). *Teachers as cultural workers.* Boulder, CO: Westview Press.

Sargent, P. (2002). Under the glass: Conversations with men in early childhood education. *Young Children, 57*(6), 22–28.

Schonpflug, U. (2009). *Cultural transmission.* New York, NY: Cambridge University Press.

ACKNOWLEDGEMENT

Lemuel W. Watson

I first would like to honor and acknowledge my mother, the late Elder Gladys Watson, for her unfathomable love and dedication to the dreams of her children. She always encouraged us to create our own paths and never doubt ourselves. Her spirit continues to console me when I am weary. I also would like to acknowledge all of the little children and their parents who had faith in me to care for their children when they had other necessary life issues. I also want to acknowledge the men in my family (Dan Watson, Lem Watson, and Lemi Hughes), who showed me what it was like to have a caring, sensitive, kind, and strong male role models to follow. Finally, I would like to thank God for giving me such an extraordinary life filled with both male and female educators who cared enough to show it.

C. Sheldon Woods

Special thanks to my late mother, Evelyn F. Woods, for her encouragement and support and her leadership in breaking race and gender stereotypes. I thank my two year old cousin, Gemarion, for reminding me of the impact that a positive male role model can have on the development of a young child. I thank the numerous male educators who paved the way, such as Mr. Armbristol, my preschool teacher. I applaud the male educators currently in the profession and welcome and encourage those males that wish to go where they belong and work with young children.

We would like to thank the educators for contributing their insights and experiences to this book.

We also wish to thank Mr. Jose O. Fernandez for all of his hard work in assisting us with this text.

LEMUEL W. WATSON

INTRODUCTION

Addressing the Culture of Gender Bias

It is becoming increasingly difficult to separate the problems of the public schools from the problems of society as a whole. Because the typical school is a mirror image of the community it serves, solutions to educational problems must likewise reflect solutions to broader social, racial, and economic problems. Men remain significantly underrepresented in elementary education and early childhood settings and in positions within the fields to make a difference regarding gender balance. In fact, according to Carrington, Tymms, and Merrell (2005) and Johnson (2008) show that male educators continue to experience bias in the hiring process; inequitable workloads, salaries and resources; and limited opportunities for growth.

We also have the tension between those advocating for more male teachers to work with children and those who are frustrated with the pace of reform. For example, there are lots of data reporting that the proportion of male teachers in schools is at it lowest in decades (National Education Association [NEA] 2003). In fact, only one of ten elementary classroom teachers is male (NEA, 2003). The literature cites multiple reasons such as the feminization of the field, low wages, social prejudice against men, lack of prestige, and social stigma are just some of the reasons for this phenomenon. Regardless of the reasons, there are debates about how to best teach children to learn. How to challenge them to be the best they can be. There is a litany of best practices, models, standards, rituals, so on and so forth as education and schooling is concerned. In some states, schools are reconsidering the fact that all children are different and need individualized instruction along with group instruction for specific subjects or skills. We are finally recognizing that perhaps a challenge to a child's learning is not the child, but the teacher, the environment, the pedagogy, the text, or the lesson plan. The debate has been long and hurtful and sometimes thought provoking. Who to educate and for what purpose has also had enough politics to fill the chambers of congress for years. The debate has also included who should teach and what qualifications should individuals have to stand before children; however, these are concerns not just for children, but "my children" and in for "my community" due to our lack of a national model or set of standards for all schools and learning.

Turning attention to the low numbers of men who work with children as a vocation is a needed and important concern. This text features a collection of research studies, scholarly essays, and personal narratives that converge on a coherent and central problem: the challenges men face in attaining, surviving, and thriving in professions that involve children, especially early childhood and elementary education.

This edited volume presents gendered research and writing on issues that influence men's experiences in early childhood and elementary education as faculty, teachers, students and academic leaders. As an advocacy work, this text aims to stimulate interest, dialogue, and collective action in creating positive and equitable working and learning environments for men who work with children. The authors include a diverse group of faculty, teachers, and administrators who have a range of experiences. They speak from experience, research, and personal opinions, across both private and public educational organizations. Their narratives and scholarship reflect a shared perspective for understanding the challenges and barriers that limit men's opportunities in vocations that work with children.

As editor, I am cognizant of the unique responsibility I have to authors and reader in allowing the voice of the author to shine through in their narrative. Here, narrative is to make sure that the reader gets enough information about the author and the purpose of their dialogue. In essence, how much does someone need to know in order to understand what is trying to be conveyed? I continue to be interested in the relationship between how the authors felt and how they made sense out of their world. According to Widdershoven (1993), who gives us the example of historians who tell stories about the past and through these stories people share about their life experiences, as a result stories become an important influence for our identity both individually and collectively. Therefore, the narratives in this book tell us who we are as men in the lives of children. "Again it can be asked what relation these stories have to the persons we are. Do they merely describe the experiences we had in the past, or are they some way constitutive for (past and actual) experience" (Widdershoven, 1993, p. 6). A question the reader might ask him or herself as they read the narratives is what is the meaning of this story and the unique issues that the writers face. All of the narratives were selected because we felt there was something to learn in addition to providing the field with some direction toward scholarship, practice, or policy. Having the authors share their experience through narratives, we learn about the cultural-historical context of the field. The authors not only share their stories about their experience and actions, they provide a mechanism for the reader to engage in a dialogue about the meaning of it all.

Widdershoven shares H. G. Gadamer's philosophical theory of interpretation from his 1960 book, Wahrheit und Method, which looks at the idea of interpretation as a dialogue that conveys the reader interprets of the text as he or she reads. In other words, interpretation through reading is a form of dialogue in which the reader and author come to terms with the issue of truth; hence this is known as fusions of horizons. This requires that we try to see what the experience has to say to us, that we try to apply it to our present situation, in simple terms, perhaps empathy.

With regards to the professional identity of the individuals and the identity as a group, male teachers, they provide for the development and construction of a bigger narrative that becomes available the field further research and practice through their shared narratives (Funkenstein, 1993). This collection of loosely biographical narrative data might be seen as life history, the subject connects and relates events, actions, and experiences with other events, actions, and experiences according to substantive and temporal patterns that do not necessarily follow the linear sequence of the 'objective time' but rather conforms to a perspectivist time model of 'subjective' or 'phenomenal' (Rosenthal, 1993 as quoted in Fischer, 1982 p. 138–215).

Given the reality there continues to be augments on both side regarding the need, benefit and relevance of men teachers in early childhood (Carrington, Francis, Hutchings, Skelton, Read, & Hall 2007; Jones, 2003), the collective voices of men who work with children on a daily basis who share their narrative give meaning to the reality in the field. "From a hermeneutic point of view, stories are based on life, and life is express, articulated, and manifested and modified in narratives" (Widdershoven, 1993, p. 9).

The stories shared through the narratives reveal the fact that to be male in early childhood is to also be cultural worker through just surviving and thriving. I believe that all teachers are cultural workers through the simple fact that teachers deal with a host of social-cultural issues through the day-to-day interactions with their pupils and their families. Male teachers, according to our authors and literature, must also deal with additional issues of gender discrimination from multiple individuals across multiple levels. The male teacher must learn very quickly how to interact to specific situation while learning the context of what is expected acceptable behavior as a male and what is not. The male teacher must become familiar with how people perceive him and understands what that means. For example, society in general still has a hard time with men being caregivers; if he is then he must be a homosexual, pervert, or weird. Hence, educating more than pupils, but the entire community and profession continues to be a challenge for the male teacher and his allies.

Finally, we have to address the issues that would divide a possible collective voice of male teachers which is the homosexual male teacher. This issue has remain silent within the teacher profession due to the fact that parents and school boards continue to be conservation given more weight to a persons sexuality than the quality of teaching and care the teacher bring to the child, school, and community. I am proud of the fact that we have narratives in this book that share openly and honestly about the challenges of gay teachers. Gay teachers are left to defend that they are not pervert or molesters in their genuine care for children. The stigma and perceptions of sexuality remains to be an issue that affects men entry into the field of early childhood. Perhaps, what is required is for all to say what does it matter if the child is learning.

Ultimately, children are the primary subject of this monograph. The "who" should teach is bigger than the gender issue. As educators we cannot excuse ourselves from responsibility in the fundamental quest for democracy and equality and how to participate in the search for its perfection (Freire, 2005). Who should teach children has to do with exposing children to differences. This difference is about what men and women of all walks of life bring to the community, schools and children's lives. The narratives of men in this text are very diverse and are all equally committed to healthy growth and development of the children they are involved with. Just as each female teacher brings gifts to the classroom so does each male teacher.

In simple terms, this book is about equal rights for men and women, who are competent, intelligent, and commitment to children and their rights to live a professional life without discrimination and prejudice for choosing such a profession. This book is about helping men go where they belong.

REFERENCES

Carrington, B., Francis, B., Hutchings, M., Skelton, C., Read, B., & Hall, I. (2007). Does the gender of the teacher really matter? Seven to eight year olds' accounts of their interactions with their teachers. *Educational Studies, 33*(4), 397–413.

Carrington, B., Tymms, P., & Merrell, C. (2005). *Role models, school improvement and the "gender gap"—Do men bring out the best in boys and women the best in girls?* EARLI 2005 conference. University of Nicosia.

Freire, P. (2005). *Teachers as cultural workers: Letter to those who dare teach.* Boulder, CO: Westview Press.

Gadamer, H. G. (1960). Tubignen, Mohr.

Funkenstein, A. (1993). The incomprehensible catastrophe: Memory and narrative. In R. Josselson & A. Lieblich (Eds.), *The narrative study of lives* (pp. 21–29). Newbury Park, CA: Sage Publication.

Johnson, S. P. (2008). The status of male teachers in public education today. Education Policy Brief. *Center for Evaluation and Education Policy, 6*(4), 1–5.

Jones, D. (2003). The right kind of man; the ambiguities of regendering the early years school environment— the case of England and Wales. *173*(6), 565–576.

National Education Association Male Teacher Fact Sheet. (2003). Retrieved June 2010, from http://www.nea.org/teachershotage/03malefactsheet.html

Rosenthal, G. (1993). Reconstruction of life stories: Principles of selection in generating stories for narrative biographical interviews. In R. Josselson & A. Lieblich (Eds.), *The narrative study of lives* (pp. 31–59). Newbury Park, CA: Sage Publication.

Widdershoven, G. A. M. (1993). The story of life: Hermeneutic perspectives on the relationship between narrative and life history. In R. Josselson & A. Lieblich (Eds.), *The narrative study of lives* (pp. 1–20). Newbury Park, CA: Sage Publication.

WILL PARNELL

1. BECOMING, BEING AND UNBECOMING AN EDUCATOR IN EARLY CHILDHOOD EDUCATION

I consider myself an educational phenomenologist, always asking questions that generate meaning in life's experiences. As I begin to write this biographical narrative, I find myself asking once again, if there are themes that run throughout my life as a male in the lives of young children. Immediately, what comes up for me is my becoming, being and unbecoming (Sumsion, 2002) in life's experiences as an early childhood educator. Sumsion (2002) suggests that this metaphor constitutes a journey, "[t]hroughout one's journey, one both shapes and is shaped by the landscapes through which one travels" (p. 3). I definitely travel through educational periods of becoming, being and unbecoming and find my way into deeply rich and meaning life experiences.

Becoming

As one of the many early childhood professionals in my area of the world, I look back and think about the unusual way I came into and stayed in this field. I see my early growth and formation in early education as my becoming educator period. During this time, I was restless, unsettled and easily influenced about arranging my classroom and career decisions.

Now, I am a professor in early childhood education at Portland State University. I also work in the full-day laboratory school for young children as the pedagogical liaison to a constructivist master's degree program, which teaches through the lab school. There, we conduct many phenomenological (Van Manen, 1990) and action research projects with children, teachers and parents of the school. People working at our school and degree program are very interested in the cross-cultural and multiple-world perspectives of early education, especially as it relates to the inspired principles and practices of Reggio Emilia, Italy (Edwards, Gandini, & Forman, 1998), anti-bias education (Derman-Sparks & the A.B.C. Task Force, 1989) and Resources for Infant Educarers (see RIE.org). Our work emerges through dialogue, collaboration, documentation and community reflection practices (Parnell, 2005). And, this work feels challenging and good most of the time!

However, way back in the day, as I was becoming an educator, I stumbled into this field as a poor work-study student at eighteen years old. I began my work part-time in the University of Oregon's off-campus housing parent cooperative school for children aged two through six. Friends had said, "Oh, you've got work-study! You should be a building guard so you can bring your books and study at your

W.Watson and C.S.Woods (eds), Go Where You Belong:
Cultural Workers in the Lives of Children, Families, and Communities, 1–10.

late-night workstation." Others suggested, "Why not work in the campus daycare center, where you can have fun and play with young children?" As I waded through the many on-campus options for work-study students, I ran across the Amazon Cooperative Preschool posting. I took their card along with many others, planning to sift through and interview. As it so happened, I interviewed with the child care director first and was hired that day to work in Amazon's cooperative preschool as a student teacher employee.

Still close to my heart and mind is my learning from Amazon Cooperative pre-school, a so-called "experimental" school (as we were termed by the housing director). We used to respond and chuckle together by saying we were a really long experiment of over twenty years. The school was an off campus housing program, affiliated with the university and used as one of the many laboratory sites across campus. I *grew up* in this vegetarian and hippy cooperative to become a teacher of young children. This was certainly a *becoming teacher* period for me, a central component to my life's formation; helping me to develop my teaching, learning and research ways in the world. I learned how to be firm and loving, have boundaries, teach through fun and exploration, conduct morning meetings, plan daily activities for various age groups, keep center schedules, discuss important topics in staff meetings, cook vegetarian meals, clean for large groups and so forth.

I also learned some hard life-lessons such as not saying to parents that their child was "manipulative," but instead letting them know how ingenious their child was at getting her needs met. Learning how to relate with multiple constituents was a life-altering experience for me. I felt like such as failure as those parents pulled their child from our program because of me. I felt as if I would never recover, but had to keep on going at the same time. The director helped me to become acutely aware of the fact that some parents do not trust schools up front; they look for a way to leave before they really even begin, and that I would grow from this experience.

I learned at Amazon that parents may leave your program and remove their children from your education and care when you aren't mindful of their perspective and aren't gracious enough to listen and promote their existence as parent and co-participant in the school through one's family experience. I learned that I could cry about the things I didn't do well, but still persevere in the face of adversity, such as when my conversation with the "manipulative-genius" child's parent did not go as planned and my put down led to her immediate withdrawal from our program.

I also learned about staff hardships and the difficulties of collaboration and listening. I learned how hard it is to work with a burned out teacher who slowly throughout the year took everything out of our room, from books and puzzles to markers and music; ultimately, neglecting the spaces by not creating a place for child-hood. On the day our director finally decided to let her go, due to much protesting from student employees and my threat to leave the program if we didn't have an intervention with my co-teacher, I opened the outdoor shed and found all of our classroom materials stuffed away.

I was mostly shocked that I had not paid enough attention to notice all of the materials missing from the classroom spaces over many months. I kept trying to make due and cover up for my co-teacher, a 35-year veteran teacher who came to us with eight letters of recommendation. My challenges with her opened my eyes to the underside of early education teaching and the control some desire to have over others. I learned to be ingenious and keep children engaged under stressed circumstances, but came up against my edge when I walked into the school early one day to find this teacher sitting on top of a child rubbing his back and saying, "We love you Chris!" While Chris firmly stating, "Get off of me!" I seemed to stay calm as I declared, "You heard his words and he was clear, now get off of him and it is time for you to go!"

As I reflect back on my becoming teacher moments, I realize that through this adversity of my co-teacher's control and my breakdown in communication with a parent I became a much stronger teacher. I resolved to be a better teacher and to give children places for play, engagement, learning and socialization, not just hollow spaces where teachers entertain children. I learned that thoughtful construction of spaces into places makes all of the difference in the flow of learning; that through this mindful construction of where and how we live in learning places, children can put their attention on great life questions such as how to peacefully negotiate for materials and spaces to create wonderment and invite big questions like how butterflies are born or what happens when you mix paint on your skin.

I grew from my first years' daze of *what did I get myself into* through *I've got power in teaching what I know* and landing on the realization that *I have so much to learn* working with parents and the community about children's educational experiences. When I graduated with a French and Italian romance language bachelor's degree, I stayed at the cooperative for one final lead-teaching year to glean and harness anything from my dynamic director. Each of the five years I was employed in the program brought me more curiously closer to the director, her family, and her ideas about relationships, joy, wisdom, and the acceptance of difference. Her dynamic engagements fostered a love and desire to carry forward this precarious *way*, which included enjoying every day and the experiences we have with one another in life. Her values reminded me of my mother, father, sister and extended family and our relationships. How our values for loving, living, communicating, and educating served as a way to raise a family amidst a community of families.

I believe that those formative years in the coop, where I was utterly accepted as a gentle person who wanted to nurture and educate children, formed my confidence to persevere even through my tough middle years. I call these years my *being educator* phase, a time when I feel secure and solid in my views of education and I begin to influence others with vision and insights. I have had so many experiences from the good to the bad and ugly in my work-world, much of it related to my gender and sexuality and society's pressures for men (me as a man) to perform manly jobs where a preschool teacher or director is not an accepted profession. Something more along the lines of my father's profession of lumberjack or my uncle's mill worker vocation would be more accepted.

3

Being

After I left Amazon, I directed an afterschool program where I would be the center of gossip by mothers out in the soccer field bleachers, worried I was going to turn their school-age children gay as if I had such power or desire to manipulate another's being in these ways. I called this *being teacher* experience the Stepford Wives phase, to relate back to Levin's (1972) satire and horror. For me, the Stepford Wives were a group of highly controlled women, whose free will and thinking was taken away, so they could please their husbands and look good to their neighbors as if keeping up appearances was of the upmost importance.

During this period, I learned that school-age program teaching and directing is the last frontier in education. We were mostly seen as after-school sitters, not as fellow educators and colleagues in the school. However, I was in a state of being, in a more comfortable place within myself as an educator and human being. I felt as if I understood the multi-layered facets to my work as a teacher and director. It was hard to shake my confidence because my self-assurance was very high. Amazon and the University of Oregon experiences had taught me to stand on my own feet and not compromise myself or my values for teaching and learning. However, I did not realize that I may have placed myself directly in harm's way, not having the protective membrane of my former accepting and caring co-workers.

While comfortable with myself and in my role, I faced many challenging events to deepen my being. In one school age program, children would look at me and say, "I don't have to listen to you, my mom's on the board and she can fire you!" In yet another, a parent demanded in a loud voice that I "get up and come over here (across a huge room) and plug this microwave in for me!" She was referring to the unplugged microwave that she wanted to use to heat up her daughter's breakfast; while I was over working with a science project at a table with a group of about seven children in the middle of pouring and mixing paints. At this stage of my career, I was in my eighth year of teaching and third of directing and I found myself longing for Amazon and my days of becoming and the safety of friendly folks. While I knew who I was, I didn't like how others were treating me. For this reason, I sought out better work places more aligned with my values and with preschool-aged children again, thinking I would find my comfort zone in a progressive preprimary school.

As my search for the right place went on, I encountered many growing pains across my career. Being a male director and hiring "younger and younger" teachers (maybe I was just getting older and older?) meant my *being educator* experiences were more about finding myself in constraining roles and power paradigms due to the attitudes of these young women coming into the field. I've encountered the label of "dad" at staff meetings such as the time when a teacher told of her difficulties and confusion of getting needs met when she goes to her "big sister" teacher and asks to purchase something; then, she is told "no" but later comes to director "dad" and is told "yes." I was the director "dad" in this scenario. I have noticed these role-labels placed on me more and more in my profession the older I get; all the while I find myself comfortable in my leadership skin, no matter what others label me. I find these labels curious more than dangerous, and I ask myself if that is how others *see and understand* me as a director. Labels lead me to wonder how else I can be tagged and what purpose these names give my profession.

I also wonder how I can exist in Beckett's (2007) notion of *in-between*, between me and the other trying to understand me, where there is pleasure in mutuality and in the unknown. I do consider what would happen if we were not able to label, but instead just exist with one another. What exists in-between me and others who try and perceive my being and my work? How could the in-between aid in weakening the old power paradigm and releasing the wall of labels that substitute for relationships? These questions have led my desire for more quality relationships, as well as they guide me and help me seek out more meaning in my experiences with others in the lives of children. Seeking out what exists in the in-between has helped me to discover more meaningful places to work and live.

After leaving the school-age world and while directing in small parent cooperative I effectively learned about children under the age of two by a team of teachers who had been together for ten years, one of whom started the school as the toddler teacher eighteen years prior to my arrival. They taught me so much and so did this parent population, filled with concerned and engaged parents. I was still a young director to most of the families, and I did not have my own children. It seemed I would often hear the dreaded, "But you don't have children so you don't understand." So, while I am seen by teachers as "dad" on the one hand, I am also "non-parent" to the parents on the other hand. These labels and roles are others' ways of attaching meaning to my educator existence, but I've rejected them periodically or sometimes played into them. I've questioned them along the way as well. I believe that they have helped me to be who others need me to be for them, which allows me to pivot in my role as an educational leader. This phenomenon has allowed me to be open and listen to others; something I think most people seek—an ear and a listener, which situates them in the in-between.

The more I've lived in *being educator*, the more tools I've acquired in my own actualization (Mazlow, 1943). An example of this revolves around some of the hardest issues I've faced with staff and parents. During my doctoral degree and about nine years into coordinating and directing at the university lab school, our school underwent an expansion and renovation. I was incredibly busy learning to teach graduate students, researching Reggio Emilia, developing practices of documentation, collaboration and reflection in the lab school, and hanging on to my co-directing role.

During this wearing period, the state of Oregon briefly opened the rights for gays and lesbians to obtain a marriage license and we had a teacher marry her partner. Being on a liberal university campus most of our community were encouraging and compassionate at their teacher's happy occasion. This teacher wanted to celebrate her marriage in the school and shared her newspaper photo with her classroom of families and children. After two years of teaching with these families, everyone already knew the teacher personally and had met her partner during a family potluck or other community event, to which the staff's family is commonly invited. Also, being in a school that takes anti-bias education seriously, we supported this teacher's right and choice to celebrate in her school community, just as any other teacher has done, no matter a person's sexual orientation. While supportive of her decision, one family was also conflicted by their religious beliefs and worried about how to broach the conflicting conversations between church and school with their four-year-old daughter.

The family wanted help to determine how to proceed with developing their religious faith in their daughter's life and the incongruent values and messages she was receiving about her teacher's life in juxtaposition with her church. The family did not approach me with their concerns, but instead went to my co-director. She took on this challenging situation by meeting with the family and taking a listening stand to aid them through their troubling internal conflict. In contrast, I was quite upset. I wanted to point out that our community would not support the biases represented by such religious beliefs and that we would want them to consider how they were hurting the teacher. Needless to say, my one-sided view was clouded by my own intolerance of a family's beliefs, which left me not wanting to listen or respond to them. I also felt righteousness in believing that our program's stance would supersede the encounters of prejudice such as those presented by this scenario. Living in a bubble does not create a healthy worldview, and I knew that I would need to grow internally to accommodate differences of beliefs and opinions, even when they directly affected me, not just a teacher in my community.

I had this nagging thought in the back of my head, one I attributed to my *being educator* phase. I kept wondering what I might have done when presented with a similar parent concern myself. What would I have done if I did not have a co-director willing to take up this problem? I felt an internal calling for my professional growth, to stretch in my thinking and to grow through my natural and comfortable way of believing.

I suddenly recognized that I had to reach into the zone of listening and seek to understand the other's point of view, even if I didn't share their same beliefs. Although I do not believe such questions about sexuality being a choice and being able to influence another's orientation by acknowledging one's own difference, I had to face real-world realities that even in my liberal community this way of thinking was alive and well and very much contrary to my own experiences in life. Having lived my entire life in a hetero-influencing culture, where the norms, images, and societal values do not support being gay or lesbian was counter to the claim that one "chooses this lifestyle" or has a "sexual preference."

In fact, I've always believed this was the way I was born and that I've always been different than the majority trying to influence me to be as they are through negative inducements such as losing family, friends, status at work, habitation, along with other social, political, and human rights enjoyed by masses of people. So instead, I found myself seeking out the positive benefits brought about by my nature, "does my being gay add to my nurturing qualities?" How can I deny my life as a gay man while working in a field that has so long supported my ability to nurture and be a gentile and loving person to children and their families? These ideas seem to go hand-in-hand in my mind and they make sense to me.

In the end, my co-director handled our particular conflict with grace, and I am still unsure of how I would have treated the matter. She listened and pointed out why we teach from a place of diversity of perspectives and countering biases. She told them that she would help them to find resources to better understand how to live with their child between two sets of values, those of church/home and of school/ community.

For me, I asked myself to stretch in my being educator. I had to move out beyond my comfort zone to transcend barriers that exist between parents, teachers and me. I had to forgive others who had transgressed against me during my *Stepford Wives* episodes and learn to believe in active listening and partnership as a way through tough work-relationship periods. I had to learn to articulate my point of view as my opinion, as something different from others who did not believe the same as me. I had to learn to live within a community which shares many points of view and welcome the other's opinions as a starting place for understanding and compassion.

I began to live in an enlightened state where mindfulness was an ongoing part of my practice at work. For me, this state of being began to look like practicing affirmations for myself that I was contented in my work-place and surrounded by people who recognized my value as an educator, a gay male educator who was impassioned with creative drive to give children the best a society and school could offer; to show the child's strength and capacity through the image of the child as inspired by the work in Reggio Emilia, Italy (Edwards et al., 1998).

Unbecoming

An unbecoming period would generally include walking away from whatever I was before, as I was formerly acting in my being educator. However, for me, unbecoming has been about releasing the old to become and be more fully in education. So, how have I released the old of my educator being, and what has this release left me with being?

I entered an educational leadership doctoral program in 2003, wanting to explore leadership at new levels. I had been a director and teacher in early childhood education for over 20 years at this point in time. I wanted to explore more education and professionally grow or I knew I would find myself leaving early education entirely. The taxing job of directing was stripping me of my desire to work with teachers, families, and children.

The educational leadership program, the major expansion and renovation of my school, and the creation of a master's specialization in early education were converging, tiring, and transformative. I began to move more and more into teacher education and away from program directing. I began to dynamically influence the pedagogy of a transforming school through teaching the teachers. In addition, I found myself shedding my old skin of being a program director to move into the new role of professor.

My unbecoming is happening simultaneously to a new becoming. As I fall away from the daily running of a school, I fall toward a tenure professor role. I think that tenure-track makes a person unravel from an old way of being. However, I'm not sure what one becomes through this process? Maybe this is the point where I stand at the precipice of someone new, not knowing or recognizing who I am or will become. It is terrifying for me. The judgment of my writing, my research, my articulation and ideas of what school means is so harsh by my peers and colleagues. I never know if others (peer-reviewers) are playing out their fantasies of having power or being the one who holds the knowledge not letting others in or if they really are trying to help me learn to better articulate my point of view, or both in a paradox; one which I cannot escape in my new vocation. I also wonder if this is part of the becoming professor for most everyone in this chosen path of becoming professor (Cooper & Stevens, 2003).

The tenure process has really taken over my life. It affects my daily existence by infiltrating the way I think about my work-life and my future in education. I love research, writing, teaching and community engagement as I disseminate my experiences and research into the world. I feel as if the constraining peer-review process has hindered my ability to fully articulate my point of view at the same time as has helped me to consider how I articulate my work for broader audiences to understand my thinking. This paradox is difficult, and I am seeking a way through to a place of calm and peace of mind. Sometimes I think I am arriving at a mindful state of being, letting go of my need to control the outcomes of my fate. At other times, I begin to unravel as I sometimes encounter the rejection and feedback that my writing, thinking or research was not accepted by the journal's reviewers for the many reasons explained, even with some conflicting opinions from reviewers.

Beyond the ups and downs of peer-review, I have internal university reviews which sometimes leave me confused. I work incredibly hard on my campus. However, my peers are mostly interested in what I've published. I receive high marks on my evaluations for every course I teach; however, my peers pressure me on how much I've published in peer-review journals. Moreover, I work fifty percent of my time at the laboratory school, designing the pedagogy of the school. I sit on two community school boards. I have designed and developed a website related to my teaching and scholarship. I help to facilitate and organize Oregon's Reggio Inspiration Network, a volunteer community organization with over 300 members. I present peer-reviewed research papers at two to three national or international education conferences each year and help my students present at local or regional conferences. I helped to create and now coordinate a master's specialization in early childhood education with over 50 students in its third year. I work with doctoral students and master's students on their research projects annually. However, my peers are most interested in underscoring my peer-reviewed publications. Their preoccupation, which is now my obsession, with publication is unraveling my experiences of living life and working with children, families and staff in early education.

Ultimately, my unbecoming educator mostly includes losing parent contact and direct experiences of learning with children. I miss this very much so as I find parents who teach me through their desires for betterment of their child's life. Children also teach me so much about living in the moment, holding on to curiosity, moving through emotions and not generally staying stuck for too long in one way of feeling and thinking about a worldview. Children are the best of human beings. They offer the world this gift as their citizenship. They are producers of a glorious way of living, not bound by all of the constraints we've put on ourselves as adults. I often wonder who makes up some of our more ridiculous rules in society; those we live by at a cost to our humanity, such as why a forty-hour work week, or why lock up food and housing is so expense? And, why we make it so hard to get along with ourselves and others.

Rinaldi (2006) says that our differences in and of themselves are not what is at stake, it is the way we treat the differences in society that is what causes us to lose our ability to listen to one another. Listening is what we are in jeopardy of losing as a fundamental factor to human relationships. Her statements undergird a new question for me. How do I stay intact and maintain the courage to go forward listening as I unravel or unbecome the old me? Is this my pathway to becoming again?

Conclusions

My crisis in the unbecoming educator is only a placeholder for what is to come next in my life. As I move through entropy and come apart at a molecular level, I realize that there is a flaw in the belief of the fatal law; the belief that all life will end in a full heat death. Instead, I have chosen to believe that as life is coming apart, there is a seed of opportunity created from the energy of breakdown. This kernel of energy allows for new life to be born from the ashes of the old. As Marx-Hubbard (1997) suggests, "Life eats entropy!" She goes on to explain that we need all of this breakdown in order to create the energy to take a quantum leap forward into the new creation of life.

I've chosen to believe in Marx-Hubbard's (1997) theory for my own reconstruction. I have encountered the random disordering time and again in my becoming, being and unbecoming processes and I have watched it turn into experiences full of meaning. With this thought in mind, I search out my copy of the book, *A Simpler Way*, by Wheatley and Kellner-Rogers (1996). I open it directly to the page on the complexity of order in life where the word emergence is significant. There is something familiar in this book to the statement of "life eats entropy" by Marx-Hubbard (1997) and it is framed around order or the emergence of life. Wheatley and Kellner-Rogers state:

> Emergence is a common phenomenon found everywhere in life. Social insects are a particularly stunning example. The tower-building termites of Africa and Australia accomplish little when they act alone; they dig only lowly piles of dirt. But as they attract other termites to their vicinity, a collective forms. As a group, they become builders of immense towers. (p. 68)

As we connect our stories with those of others, we find we can build immense towers, bridges to understanding and meaningful moments in the in-between. I wish life experiences will help me to grow and become a better person in order to influence the lives of the most wonderful of humans, the lives of young children. This grand desire creates a reordering of my life's priorities and develops a more complex way of seeing into the world. It also carries with it the struggle for meaning and the complexity of identity reconstruction and intense listening that is required of each human being working in teaching and learning.

In the end, as a man in the lives of young children, I challenge others to deeply consider and reflect on their own experiences with our youngest. Who do we want to be when we are standing in front of the best of human beings? Will we begin the labels game? Or, will we seek to live in the in-between where the good rises up into strong and unmediated relationships? I believe that to create this space requires a will to want to stop, pay attention, deeply listen, and generate doubt and the precariousness we feel when encountering one another.

REFERENCES

Beckett, C. J. (2007). *Playing in the In-between: Implications for early childhood education of new views of social relations.* Ph.D. thesis, University of New South Wales, Kensington. NSW, Australia.
Cooper, J. & Stevens, D. (2003). *Tenure in the sacred grove. Issues and strategies for women and minorities.* New York: SUNY Press.
Derman-Sparks, L., & the A.B.C. Task Force (1989). Anti-bias curriculum: Tools for empowering young children. Washington, DC: National Association for the Education of Young Children.
Edwards, C., Gandini, L., & Forman, G. (1998). *The hundred languages of children: The Reggio Emilia approach-Advanced reflections* (2nd ed.). Greenwich, CT: Ablex.
Levin, I. (1972). *The stetford wives.* New York: Random House.
Marx-Hubbard, B. (1997). *Conscious evolution (Cassette tape).* Wilsonville, OR: Living Enrichment Center.
Maslow, A. H. (1943). A theory of human motivation, *Psychological Review, 50*(4), 370–396.
Parnell, Will. (2005). Teacher learning: Documentation, collaboration, and reflection. *Dissertation Abstracts International, 67*(5), 186A. (UMI No. 3218144).
Rinaldi, C. (2006). *In dialogue with Reggio Emilia: Listening, researching and learning.* New York: Routledge.
Sumsion, J. (2002). Becoming being, and unbecoming an early childhood educator: A phenomenological case study of teacher attrition. *Teaching and Teacher Education, 18,* 869–885.
Van Manen, M. (1990). *Researching lived experience: Human science for an action sensitive pedagogy.* Albany, NY: State University of New York Press.
Wheatley, M., & Kellner-Rogers, M. (1996). *A simpler way.* San Francisco: Berrett-Koehler Publishers, Inc.

DARRELL C. HUCKS

2. A TALE OF COLLECTIVE ACHIEVEMENT

When I first started teaching public school in New York City over a decade ago, I was concerned with how I would be perceived as an African American male elementary school teacher in a climate where most of the teachers in public schools were, and still are, white females. I will never forget when I was a student teacher at the same school the year before one morning a visibly shaken Latina mother approached me as I was taking down desks off the tables saying, "I know this is a progressive school and all, but I have to draw the line at this." She handed me what appeared upon first glance to be the classified section of a local newspaper that was filled with ads of naked women (except for strategically placed black dots covering certain parts of their anatomy) and I looked at her with a puzzled look. She then told me that her son—who had come into the classroom a few minutes before she arrived and was, at the moment, on the other side of the classroom at the lizard tank in the science area—was looking at these pages of ads at their home and he told her that I had given it to him.

My concern about being a male teacher quickly began to take on nightmare proportions. Well, without missing a beat, I called the student, and he began to walk over slowly, head hanging low—the walk of guilt. It didn't take much questioning before he revealed through tears that he had lied to her. His mother said, "Oh my God, Darrell, I'm so sorry." I told her, "I would never..." and before I could finish my sentence she began to give him a verbal spanking, letting him know that he could have gotten me in some serious trouble and had him apologize to us both. That moment taught me how important—no, sacred, it is to build trusting relationships with children's families and that you have to be honest and understanding—and fully present. I ended up teaching her daughter for three years during my subsequent time as a teacher at the same school and this mother was one of my strongest supporters. Years later, thanks to the internet, we are all still in contact today. Both her children are attending college and are doing well.

In my eyes, my real development as an educator actually began on the last day of class of my first year teaching public school. I was struggling to hold back the emotions of having to say goodbye to the twenty-four children that I had come to care for deeply. It was a year that started off full of hopes and dreams by any new teacher. The summer before I began teaching was spent dreaming of what my classroom would look like and sound like. I imagined happy, worry-free children reading books, drawing pictures, and playing learning games. In preparation for making this dream a reality, I would frequently hop into my little Honda Civic that summer

W.Watson and C.S.Woods (eds), Go Where You Belong:
Cultural Workers in the Lives of Children, Families, and Communities, 11–19.

and storm teacher supply stores. My favorite place to shop was one located in an outer borough of New York City. I remember walking into what appeared to be a sprawling suburban supermarket complete with four-wheeled shopping carts, the only difference was that this store was not filled with produce, meats, and aisles of colorfully packaged canned-goods—it was filled with posters, board games, mathematics and science materials, and seemingly every workbook known to mankind. I would roam up and down the aisle grabbing items to put in my cart that caught my eye—sometimes, without even checking the price. After loading up the trunk of my car with my latest bounty of school supplies, I would drive back to NYC, still dreaming.

I was young and determined, and I wanted to have the perfect first year. So, when I transported my purchases to my classroom on the third floor of the school, upon entering the room, I immediately noticed that the "horrible" magenta and brown walls were not in keeping with my "perfect classroom" dream, and I quickly approached the principal of my school to ask for permission to paint the walls of my classroom. "Sure" and a smile was what I received in response, and off I went with credit card in hand. I learned from one of my graduate courses that the most learning-conducive color for a classroom for children was something like a school-bus yellow—my dream was another step closer to being a reality.

Well, by the time I made it from the first floor to the doorway of my classroom with freshly mixed cans of paint, the telephone in my empty classroom began to ring. I answered and it was the principal of my school asking me to come down to the main office on the second floor to talk to her for a second. She sat me down and told me that I couldn't paint my classroom and the ultimate decision was out of her hands. Again, I was young, determined, and naïve with minimal background on the politics of the public school system and public school buildings. "It's ok, I'll use the paint (formidable expensive Benjamin Moore) for something else." I stored it away on the very bottom shelf of my classroom closet and sat on the bench in my class-room looking at those "horrible" walls and decided to strategically hang big Day-Glo flowers on the walls—in combination with the posters and other items I'd purchased, my room would still be eye-catching and festive for my future first and second grade students. I was determined to have my own "Martha Stewart moment" on that first day of school.

So there I was on that sunny September morning with a smile on my face, expecting that my little first and second graders would be so happy that they had such a cool looking classroom. It wasn't until after morning meeting, about an hour into the school day watching children who were more focused on each other than the classroom walls, I realized that when I was putting together my classroom it was from the perspective of a 6 foot 2 inch tall man's and not from the perspective of the average height of a first or second grader. Well, I spent the next couple of hours at the end of the day lowering everything that I could to their level of vision.

That year, I listened to the "experienced wisdom" of my fellow teachers at my non-traditional school and kept my students happy playing games, drawing, painting, encouraging invented spelling, and choice-time made up a large portion of our day. For a while it seemed like we celebrated the drop of a pencil with cupcakes and juice in my classroom—I wanted my students to enjoy school. My assigned mentor,

a fellow teacher with years of "experienced wisdom," would come to observe me from time to time teaching a lesson that I had prepared, and as I taught, I noticed her meandering around my classroom checking the markers in the containers at each table by rubbing them on a blank sheet of paper. When she grabbed the first marker,
I thought she was getting ready to take some copious notes on my lesson, but I was mistaken. Her feedback consisted of a somewhat begrudgingly: "That was good." while handing me a couple of markers, "These are dry!" Then advising me to replace them as she walked out and back to her own classroom. The word "hazing" comes to mind now. I remember staff meetings where the focus seemed to be either how "delicious" or, on the opposite end of the spectrum, how "emotionally disturbed" students were. Looking back on those times now it seems like we rarely spoke about children's academic development in comparison to the large amount of time we spent discussing their emotional and social development.

So on that last day of my first year of teaching, my students and I celebrated the end of the school year with pizza, music, and dancing. When the last student hugged me good-bye that hot June afternoon, I returned to that bench in my classroom that I'd sat at months before dreaming of what my first year would be like, and I sobbed. No, these were not tears of joy at my accomplishment of surviving my first year in the classroom, not tears about the fact that I would miss them—and I would, without question. No, I cried because I asked myself one question on that bench, "What did I teach them?" and the tears flowed because I couldn't answer it with any conviction or real proof. I vowed at that moment that as long as I was a teacher this would be a question that I would be able to answer yearly, monthly, weekly, daily, moment to moment, and to each individual child.

At the time, I felt that I had not "done right"; that is, done my best by the children that I had grown to love and had grown to love me. I had not done right by their families who were entrusting me with their care and well-being. I began to realize upon reflection that "I'd put my good sense on the shelf" (as my mother used to say) that first year and listened to the "hazers." Although I didn't always agree with them, I was an insecure first-year teacher. Still, it wasn't like I didn't know who my students were; it wasn't like there was some pre-existing cultural discontinuity or divide between us. I identified with my Black and Latino students, many of whom came from neighborhoods like the one I had grown up in as a child in the Bronx. Their families were like my friends' families—like my Bronx neighbors. Actually, watching them was like watching my self as a child. The urgency to rectify this experience for me as a teacher had to do with the fact that I knew how important these childhood years were and that they were irreplaceable and precious—they were the foundational year. Rising off that bench I vowed, "Never again!" would I let this happen to me or my students.

But as fate would have it, I was asked to "loop up" for the upcoming school year to teach the next grade with many of the same students. I saw it as divine intervention and a chance to "get it right." I spent the next summer taking graduate education courses, and definitely not spending too much time and money at the teacher supply stores. I reflected on the things that I thought I did well as a teacher and the areas that

I needed to improve. But most of all, I thought about my students—each one of them—what did they need? What had I learned from them? Then I thought about my own childhood teachers, what had they done that worked? What were the things that didn't seem to work and why? The questions came and so did some of the answers.

Ironically, the most powerful learning experience that summer was a brief vacation trip to India. While I was there, I visited a school in a small fishing village and once the news spread through the village that I was a teacher, I was invited by some of the school's teachers to visit the village school. I remember thinking how similar the children were in NYC to children in the fishing village, when I approached the school I saw young children my students' age at recess playing with cars and trucks that were individually attached to a long string. So as one child pulled the pint-sized vehicle, the others chased behind laughing and smiling. But upon closer inspection, I realized that the cars and trucks that I dismissed as "just like the ones my kids had," were actually small colored-boxes with no wheels at all. When I was invited into the school to meet the teachers, they were warm and friendly, but the classroom was not like mine at all. It had a dirt floor, bare stone walls and an old small chalkboard.

Then the teacher asked if I would lead the class in an English lesson and handed me a workbook that had seen better days. I smiled and moved up front and with no "Eat at Joe's" environmental distractions, I turned my attention squarely to the children. They were sitting not at tables or desks but next to each other on a few wooden pews—their eyes locked on me. As I went over the story and the vocabulary word fill-ins on the page, I transported us all, in my mind, to my classroom with all its "Eat at Joe's" accoutrements and began to immediately imagine their heads turning away from me—their eyes looking for distraction. It was at that moment that I realized that part of the reason that urban students, in particular Black and Latino boys, were labeled with attention deficit (hyperactivity) disorder (ADD/ADHD) had more to do with the environment and less to do with them. It had more to do with how and what they are taught to pay attention to and less about an inability to focus. If ten or more things are competing for my attention at the same time, then how can I possibly focus on one of them for any length of time? I was inspired by the teachers and the learners in the poor fishing village in India. Especially by two fourth graders at that school, who were building a scale model of the school out of paper, outside of their school principal's office. They had simple rulers, no bells and whistles-materials like the children in many schools in NYC, yet the work they produced was of the highest quality. My mind pondered how these village children with next to nothing were so focused, so intelligent, so engaged. While in many of New York's public schools, children were basically tripping over books and materials daily, yet many of them were unfocused and struggling academically in school.

Fueled by my experience in India, the following September my second and third grade students walked into a classroom that was not riddled with pre-made posters and charts—I left some of the flowers. I explained to them that when we put things up on the walls, it's because we decided that we need it for our work. They got it and suddenly all those decorative extras disappeared and only reappeared if it related to the teaching and learning that occurred. So we went from "Eat at Joe's" to

"Let's Build Joe's"—it was powerful. I taught them as if my life and theirs were at stake—they were. I knew that these urban children didn't stand a chance unless I got them to work at and beyond what the academic standards for their grade suggested. My goal was to provide them with the tools they needed to dream their futures and still dream my own future as a new teacher. Knowing that what I was about to do would rub some people the wrong way—mainly the "hazers," I planned how to better address their academic needs in progressive ways by shaping a curriculum that mixed the "tried and true" with the new.

As I reinvested in the power of education to transform lives, I reinvested in the art of teaching and the gift of learning. I took strategies into my classroom that I'd learned from the renowned teacher education school I was attending for my master's degree at the time. I adapted and differentiated instruction based on my students' needs sometimes a day or two after I had learned a method in a particular course and gave feedback to my professors and classmates at our next class meeting. Some of my students resisted these changes and my high expectations, especially those who had been at the school since kindergarten and had become use to being engaged based upon their social and emotional whims—where opting out of learning at times was allowed. I was focused on their academic development from that moment on. In the beginning of this period of change in my teaching, I found myself having to revisit classroom management and behavioral issues regularly. There would be no more "time outs" for students who were horse-playing or engaging in off-task behavior. Children at my school were often sent to "visit" other classrooms or the principal's office for misbehavior. Now, things were different; the only option for my students was "time in" with me. In other words, my expectation was that I would give them a few in-class minutes/seconds to get themselves together because they were not leaving the classroom. I would often say to students who early on asked to leave the classroom for unacceptable reasons, "absolutely not. I am not teaching in the hallway or the principal's office. You are a part of this learning community and we are expecting you to contribute to our learning by focusing on your work and not disturbing our community. We need you here with us." Overtime, this mantra took effect and we got down to the business of learning and the horse-play and requests stopped.

Another turning point I experienced a few years later was taking my students out of the classroom. For example, I discovered that two of the older boys who were previously slated to receive special services before they became my students, were picked up by the special education teacher and taken to his room. As fate would have it, I was on a prep and went to check to see how they were doing with the writing assignment I gave and were supposed to be working on with the assistance of the special education teacher. To my surprise, I found this particular teacher sitting at his desk on one side of the room completely lost in the pages of the *New York Times*. My two students sat a distance away playing with two action figures, there notebooks nowhere in sight. I took them and their notebooks with me back to my classroom, leaving the special education teacher still lost in his newspaper. He didn't even notice that I entered the room. With a finger to my lips and a sweeping motion, they quietly got up and left with me. I quietly closed the door behind me.

It actually took over five minutes for the teacher to show up at my classroom door. After a conversation with my school's principal, I made sure that he never took another one of my students out of my classroom again, but he was always welcome to come in and work with them in my classroom. No matter where my students would go, recess or lunch, I went too. I tried to find out if they behaved differently in different contexts. More important, I wanted to support them in their activities and inform my teaching; an informed teacher is an effective teacher.

The constant observation of my students reinforced at the time, the importance of staying informed about the work of my colleagues. I would frequently visit the art, movement, and gym teachers' classrooms when my students were with them. Not necessarily to check on the teachers, but to build on our work with the children. I also encouraged these same teachers to come visit my classroom. This often led to the development of collaborative projects that further enhanced the learning experiences of my students, and our professional development as teachers.

I was relentless and transparent with my students. I would tell them what I expected now and how I expected them to handle their responsibilities as my students. I affectionately referred to them as "my babies"; they loved it. I was inspired by my educator role models such as Lorraine Monroe, Lisa Delpit, and many others. I built relationships with each student and facilitated their building of constructive and supportive relationships with each other. We were not only a team but a family of learners. It was not uncommon for a child to have posed a question to me with, "Daddy (and sometimes, humorously) Mommy this or that…" to which I would smile and respond "Yes, son or yes, my child." We'd share a laugh and keep working. They knew I loved them. I told them regularly and without hesitation, both girls and boys. For many, I wasn't just their teacher but the nurturing father figure they may not have had. But they were all clear about my role as their teacher, and their roles as students. I was not a peer or a friend; I was a caring responsible adult. Mutual respect was of the utmost importance to me.

I told my students that I would speak to them the same way, in the same tone (especially, if I was being stern at the time) in front of their parents as I was speaking to them in the moment. I learned that some children played with their hard-working parents emotions, and for attention they would inflate reprimands at school to make themselves look like the victims of a cruel or insensitive teacher. Parents, who feel guilty for not always being able to be around for their children due to work, fall for this tactic, and it could lead to confusion and resentment, and sometimes, confrontations between home and school. I knew that my students' success was directly tied to keeping the lines of communication between home and school open and active. Parents could call me at home and on my cell phone, and I made sure that I had their contact numbers as well. I called most often to share positive news about their child's development as a learner and sometimes to share a concern. I also sent home notes of praise to parents regarding their child's accomplishments. An informed parent is a trusting parent.

Over time, many of my conversations with parents were about them seeking my advice on managing their child's behavior at home and outside of school, and we worked things out together. The running jokes among my students were that I had cameras watching them at home when they left me at the end of the school day, or that I slept at the school, or never slept at all. What they didn't realize is that their parents would share their lives with me on a regular basis. I learned about families' weddings, trips, birthdays, and occurrences that may have happened to or from school. When I learned about the death of a loved one in one of my students' families, I offered a shoulder to cry on if needed. We were a big extended family, and it was common for my students to request that we spend the night or weekend at school. Their families were welcomed into our classroom to work with us at anytime. An emotionally safe learning environment is an engaging and effective learning environment.

Over the years, my students' attendance records were outstanding. I will never forget the day when the "attendance woman" from the Department of Education came to my classroom to meet me and shake my hand. She said, "I don't know what you're doing but your kids are never absent." I responded, "Yes, they like school." Honestly, parents would tell me that even when their children were really sick and bed-ridden they would be upset about missing school. That was a huge testament to our co-constructed learning environment because the children worked hard and their achievement on formal and informal assessments was off the charts. We did not do drill and kill test prep sessions everyday either, but I embedded test-taking strategies into my progressive teaching methods and pointed out connections across the curriculum to them regularly, reminding them of connections to something that we learned yesterday or even a year ago. I encouraged them to speak up when they didn't understand something; that was their job! And yes, we celebrated their achievements with the same frequency and vigor as we did holidays and birthdays. I wanted to convey that learning and achievement should be acknowledged and praised. In my eyes, I was only an effective teacher if they were effective learners.

Overtime, some of the "hazers" became "haters" but it didn't bother me. I was there for the children and managed to build some very supportive collegial relationships despite being in a climate where, at one time, I was once told by another peer that it wasn't fair to the other teachers in our school that my class was so high functioning. The comment packed a wallop because it came from someone I trusted at the time and respected as a colleague; however, I let it go and held on to my high expectations of myself, my students and the school. Sometimes raising your standards means that people around you have to raise theirs. I began to see that change happening at my school. Our professional development meetings were being spent on sharing academic development strategies as well as socio-emotional development strategies. We began to look at the connections within grade levels and across grade levels in our school. It was around this time that I made the decision to leave the elementary classroom to pursue doctoral studies in education. I wanted to reach more children and be an agent of change on a systemic level.

After recently finishing my doctoral degree a few years ago, I still find myself in the classroom. Now my students are future teachers enrolled in teacher education programs at a major university. By working with the next generation of public school teachers, I'd like to think that I am being an agent of change in the lives of even more children than before. Most of my current students are still majority white females and most of their public school students will be majority Black and Latino. So my mission is to get them ready to touch the lives of these children in positive ways give them the theoretical, practical, culturally responsive, and self-reflective tools they need to help their future urban students dream their future.

My years teaching young children have helped to shape my own research agenda. The research study I conducted for my doctoral dissertation was a qualitative study of the cross-generational schooling experiences of African American males. I interviewed elementary school age boys and older males in their immediate and extended family to find out what school was like from their perspectives and how would their experiences inform the educational system that continues to host them in the bottom tiers of academic achievement. What do these voices say about the challenges they face and more importantly do their voices say about the existing statistical data may not capture?

The narrative stories of the African American males participating in this study, across the generations, reveal a common thread about education. It is multifaceted and it involves the work of many—students, parents, community members, administrators, etc. Upon analysis of these narratives, simply put, good schooling is invested in collective achievement and bad schooling is not invested in collective achievement.

Most of the males in the study have experienced more of the later. Regardless of age, they were clearly able to articulate and extrapolate what teaching that is invested in collective achievement should look like. It is caring, filled with high expectations; it is resourceful; it is culturally responsive; it is dynamic; it is connected and builds on other stakeholder contributions, and it doesn't matter who is doing it male, female, Black or White, etc. And most importantly, according to the youngest participants in this study—it should be fun. Ladson Billing's work on culturally responsive curriculum and pedagogy provided a framework for reforming teacher education and impacting student achievement for marginalized students. Collective achievement builds on her seminal work and offers another framework that will reach not only students and teachers, but all stakeholders in and outside the classroom.

The question we must ask ourselves is: should students' academic trajectory be predetermined by the assumptions and beliefs that teachers have of students, their families, and their communities? No, but it happens everyday in schools, based on teachers' perceptions of the educational legacy and experiences that are passed on generation to generation that enters the classroom with each student they teach. The demographics of the majority who are teaching in public school classrooms today are white, middle-class females, in contrast to students they teach, who are students of color. Again, what assumptions do teachers make because of differences of race, ethnicity, gender and class? How do teachers view and respond to the educational legacies that walk into schools and classrooms each day? These are critical questions that teachers and schools must ask.

This year I will be attending the high school graduations of many of my former elementary school students, and I will be just as proud of them on that day as I was when they graduated from the school I taught. I was an elementary school teacher in a large urban public school system for several years prior to pursuing my doctoral studies. A few years ago, I attended the eighth grade graduation ceremony of my former third grade students. After the ceremony, I found myself locked in a warm embrace with a former student and his family. As we shared in this moment of celebration, this African American mother said to me, "You did it, you should be so proud. Look at what you've done, all your hard work." Still hugging them, I said, "No, look at what *we've* done." Now, through the lens of my research, I see that moment as a defining moment of collective achievement. In lifting each of their roles, I then addressed my own. I told his mother she got him ready for school everyday and every time she attended class conferences. I reminded the father about the time when he read books with his son on the bus to and from school. I shared with his aunt how she helped him with his homework after school. And to the student I said, "You worked hard and wanted to learn." I was able to do my work because from the start I acknowledged and incorporated their work with my own. On that graduation day, I shared in many moments such as this that I now see as key examples of collective achievement. These moments continue to resonate in my head and have helped me put the pieces together, in concert with the literature, and most definitely with the voices of the African American males in my study.

In examining the schooling experiences and achievement of African American males, educators and researchers have often not viewed them as being knowledgeable informants of their own experiences. Contrary to this approach, I asked African American boys and men to share their schooling experiences with me and they did. My participants taught me about how they negotiate their identity as African American males and navigate the terrain of availability and access to opportunity regarding their education. These are voices of experience that can inform the work of educators, administrators, researchers, parents, community organizations, and policy-makers. Collective achievement is a model of reciprocity. As teachers and students our fates are linked. It breeds shared responsibility and shared accountability.

SHAUN JOHNSON

3. A NEW PERSPECTIVE ON THE LACK
OF MEN IN EDUCATION

Three elementary teachers walk into a bar—two men and one woman—to enjoy some happy hour libations after a long day in professional development meetings. The teachers in question are relatively young in contrast to their colleagues. Duties of family and marriage are barely on the horizon, so they try to maintain a few youthful rituals of their lives prior to teaching. That is, cheaper drinks at a local watering hole after a long day at work still have some cachet. The conversation is fairly typical for teachers who have been unleashed. There is talk of the most annoying children or perhaps a diatribe against the soporific slog of full staff meetings.

One of the guys, a fourth grade teacher, begins a long and familiar soliloquy about not being able to find the perfect woman in his life. His two companions commenced reassurances as soon as this cry for help was completed. There were many laughs to be had, until the one female in the group interjected, "Well, you guys are screwed no matter what." To this statement, the other male, who has been a silent and sympathetic listener up to this point, replied with a very cautious, "Why?" She reasoned, "You're teachers. There is no way you could afford a woman."

What started off as a joke turns out to be a true story, something that I experienced as a former fifth grade teacher. To be clear, I was not the one with the relationship troubles. But the fact that this happened evinces problems on several levels. On a broad scale, the anecdote proves that varying degrees of sexism persist in mainstream society. Sexism in this case is demonstrated by my former colleague's restrictive view of masculinity: traditional gender roles demanded that we as men bring home the proverbial bacon. Our meager teacher salaries would make us unlikely candidates as domestic patriarchs. Thus, we were shirking our responsibilities as primary bread-winners, screwed as it were, according to our female colleague's post-margarita patois, and condemned to perpetual bachelorhood.

The fact that male educators experience pejorative comments because they chose to work with children and young people is only one very specific symptom of sexism within mainstream society along with domestic abuse, rape and sexual assault, and the persecution of the lesbian, gay, bisexual, and transgender (LGBT) community. I am in no way deluded into thinking that a few "identity bruises" (Foster & Newman, 2005) suffered by male teachers is a crisis of these proportions. I will, however, argue throughout this text that casting aspersions towards men who teach, or any male who violates a culturally defined ideal of manhood, is evidence of a problem for which

W.Watson and C.S.Woods (eds), Go Where You Belong:
Cultural Workers in the Lives of Children, Families, and Communities, 21–32.

teachers and other education professionals have a direct responsibility in eliminating. If it is reasonable to assume that teachers are cultural mediators who inculcate their students with a certain set of values, then education as a social institution is on the frontlines of combating sexism, misogyny, and homophobia.

In this chapter, I will draw from my experiences as a male, former elementary teacher, and currently as an education researcher to make some important distinctions between the *problem* of male teachers and the enveloping *conversation* regarding its potential solutions. I will also identify a few problems with the prevailing discussion on the lack of male teachers and suggest an alternative discourse that may give educators and reformers a better chance at actually solving the inclusivity problem in teaching.

Problem and Conversation

My research and teaching experiences revealed both the male teacher *problem* and an overall *conversation* on the lack of men in education. First, the *problem* posed by a dearth of men in the classroom has two important levels. On the one hand, it is quite obvious that there are far fewer men in teaching than women. The Bureau of Labor Statistics (BLS) certainly corroborates this view, which reported in 2007 the percentage of male teachers at various educational levels: postsecondary (53.8%), secondary (43.1%), elementary and middle school (19.1%), and preschool (2.7%). The National Education Association (NEA) in their most recent estimates puts the overall proportion of male teachers at roughly 24 percent. The statistical nature of the problem, however, is not endemic to the United States. Data from the United Nations Educational Social and Cultural Organization (UNESCO) from 2005, for instance, shows a similar gender disparity in teaching within every major developed country in the world.

The second aspect of the male teacher *problem* is a bit more complicated: the gender disparity contradicts public education's mission of promoting democratic values, namely equity, equal opportunity, and egalitarianism. To follow this up with a question, why do we continue sending our children to schools that seem to promote the sexist message that men rule women and women rule children (Gutmann, 1987)? Schools are important sites of cultural reproduction or, to use Connell's (1988) term, "agents of socialization" (p. 191). As such, they play a key role in shaping children's attitudes towards all matters of diversity, whether it is gender, race, class, or sexual orientation. If larger cultural forces discourage men from working with children for a variety of reasons, are schools and its professional workforce failing in their roles as arbiters of democratic values? Comfort with care, child welfare, and mentoring young people are valuable precursors of the desire to teach (Bastick, 2000; Drudy, Martin, Woods, & O'Flynn, 2005; Hansen & Mulholland, 2005; Smedley & Pepperell, 2000). It would thus behoove educators to prime men in this role earlier in their lives and without recrimination ensure perhaps a more permanent resolution to the various levels of the male teacher problem.

In terms of the *conversation* surrounding male teachers, this refers to the tone of discourse on the problem and its potential solutions. The empirical literature on male teachers is primarily committed to describing the unique obstacles that men face within the profession (see, for example, Coulter & McNay, 1993; Cushman, 2005; DeCorse & Vogtle, 1997; Francis & Skelton, 2001; Frank & Martino, 2006; Goodman & Kelly, 1988; King, 1998; Mills, Martino, & Lingard, 2004; Montecinos & Nielson, 2004; Roulston & Mills, 2000; Sargent, 2001; Skelton, 2003; Smedley & Pepperell, 2000; Sumison, 1999). Another portion of the literature speculates a prioiri if the male teacher problem is even worth exploring considering teacher gender's dubious influence on a variety of student attitude and outcome measures (Bricheno & Thornton, 2007; Carrington, Tymms, & Merrell, 2005; Driessen, 2007; Gold & Reis, 1982; Lahelma, 2000; Paradise & Wall, 1986; Tsouroufli, 2002).

There is, however, a more mainstream commentary on the lack of men in education that is largely based on two problematic assumptions, the first of which is the dubious presence of ongoing male underachievement, dubbed the "boys crisis" by both its proponents and its critics. This is part and parcel of the conversation on gender and education that has recently shifted from the needs of girls to boys (Weaver-Hightower, 2003).

Numerous texts have been published mainly for a mainstream audience whose ultimate purposes are to ratchet up parental fears about a crisis of male under-achievement due to an overemphasis on the needs and educational equity for girls over the last few decades (e.g., Hoff-Summers, 2000; Sax, 2006; Tyre, 2008). A major problem with these texts is that they are not rigorously researched and do not rely on the robust body of literature on gender and education that already exists. An additional problem concerns the assumption that a "boys crisis" is actually occurring. Achieve-ment data is notoriously ambiguous and crisis proponents rarely take into account both unequal distributions of social power and other complicating factors like race and class (Anderson & Accomando, 2002; Mac an Ghaill, 1996; Mills & Keddie, 2007).

The second problematic assumption of the prevailing conversation on male teachers concerns role modeling. I do not imply that role modeling is not an important function of our schools or that teachers are not effective role models. There are a few reasons, however, why role-modeling discourse in its current form may reaffirm the cultural stereotypes that work against male participation in teaching. First, it is challenging to even define role modeling. Sargent (2001) in his discussions with male teachers found their descriptions of role modeling for boys devoid of specific details and stunningly "colorless and vague and [lacking] any sense of being pro-active" (p. 118). There is also no strong evidence that children even look to their teachers as role models; moreover, Bricheno and Thornton (2007) found that elementary students largely do not.

Finally, "boys crisis" proponents in particular argue that there are certain characteristics of masculinity that must be modeled, especially given the fears over the breakdown of the traditional family. Who gets to define what features are modeled and is it not restrictive definitions of masculinity defined by fantasy and not reality actually the problem? Additionally, there is abundant evidence from the research literature that male teachers may actually reinforce rather than challenge sexist stereotypes (DeCorse & Vogtle, 1997; Goodman, 1987; Jamison, 2000; Lewis,

Butcher, & Donnan, 2006; Montecinos & Nielsen, 2004; Roulston & Mills, 2000; Skelton 2003). Simply because male teachers are transformative figures on the surface does not mean that they are individually sensitive to the conditions that promote their continued absence. It is essential then that the kind of role modeling occurring in the classroom challenge the sexist and homophobic values that contribute to the disparities in the teaching profession.

An Alternative Commentary

From all the reading and research I have done on male teachers, I do believe that it is still a problem, but not for reasons one might initially expect. In our collective enthusiasm to encourage more men to teach, we must first be careful not to devalue the work of millions of women teachers by uncritically valorizing the caring that men do (Francis, Skelton, Carrington, Hutchings, & Read, B., 2008; Gaskell & Mullen, 2006). We must also be careful to avoid cultural stereotypes in the efforts to recruit more male teachers, such as emphasizing coaching opportunities as a perk of the job. Mainstream calls for more male teachers based on male underachievement and role modeling violate both of these principles. First, accepting the idea that male teachers are necessary because their gender achieves some sort of balance in the classroom or school, the two-category framework of gender, or categoricalism, is preserved. This also implies that children require exposure to two different options in order to develop their own healthy gendered identities. Is it not a simple categorical approach to gender that is a primary cause of the lack of male teachers? Second, focusing heavily on the fear and suspicion surrounding male care giving, extolling the men who teach despite the scrutiny still normalizes female care giving and celebrates the men without acknowledging the actual quality of their teaching.

To avoid problematic concepts that may contribute to the idea that teaching is not for men, I suggest a new commentary on male teachers that is responsive to the systemic social and cultural factors that discourage their participation in care giving roles. This alternative conversation is based on two innovative concepts from the research on gender, education, and democracy: *multiple subjectivities* and *inclusivity of difference*. I will walk the reader through each of them.

In terms of *multiple subjectivities*, the central motive force behind this concept is "hegemonic masculinity," a sociological construct developed extensively by Australian social theorist Connell (1988, 1995), whose work is mentioned frequently in this text. The maxim that a dominative form of masculinity exists that, through a complex web of social, political, economic, and institutional forces, marginalizes other men and subordinates women leaves the door open to an exciting proposition: that multiple forms of masculine subjectivities exist apart from the cultural ideal constantly espoused in the media and defended by social norms. In defiance of the ideal, certain men can "protest" hegemonic masculinity by engaging in practices that challenge conventional norms (Connell, 1995). To pluralize masculinity to "masculinities" is a simple grammatical change, yet a huge conceptual leap for many people traditionally accustomed to the essentialist categories of man and woman. Some kind of structure for resistance needs to be established in order to usher in a greater recognition of a pluralized masculinity.

It is one thing to acknowledge that there are multiple ways to practice one's gender, but it must also be followed up by ensuring that society actively promotes an *inclusivity of difference*. That is, the removal of any social hierarchy that legitimizes one practice of gender over another. Specifically regarding masculinity, for example, excessive consumption of meat products, a custom of traditional manhood, is not valued any more highly than an affinity for arugula, the effete salad green highlighted in the 2008 Presidential election to "feminize" Barack Obama. Maloutas (2006) argues that democracy is more than a political structure. It must be "a cultural frame-work which should primarily determine the inter-subjective relations in the so-called private sphere. This necessarily presupposes radical changes in how gender is perceived, changes which entail rejection of any dichotomous/hierarchical logic" (p. 72). Thus, democratic values in governance must be additionally transmutable to cultural values, or how we live our social lives within a democracy. To create a gender-inclusive society, the power of the people to govern themselves instantaneously translates to the power of all gendered subjectivities to access equal opportunities without recrimination.

Progressive Challenges

A spate of recent research literature on the lack of men in education is already embracing language and ideas consistent with my suggested alternative commentary. This work has also been for some time setting up progressive challenges to the more conservative assumptions inherent to the "boys crisis" and calls for male teachers based on role modeling and male underachievement. I would like to take some time in the following section to acknowledge what exemplars of this progressive research is trying to do for the male teacher conversation. The reader may notice, however, that much of this work is being done overseas, so I cannot emphasize enough how important it is for these ideas to reach our shores and into the mainstream discourse on men in education.

Commandeering the Boys

Several empirical studies attempt to quash various crisis hypothesis, namely that "boys" can be treated as one monolithic group with similar problems (Francis & Skelton, 2005; Gorard, Rees, & Salisbury, 1999; Martino, Lingard, & Mills, 2004; Mead, 2006; Mills & Lingard, 2007; Mills, Hasse, & Charlton, 2008). Indeed, the capture of the public imagination of crisis rhetoric is owed to "its ability to over-simplify highly complex situations, forecast danger, and attribute blame" (Titus, 2004, p. 158). Schools and teachers are the easiest targets of parental ire when it comes to their boys. A constant project then for the literature is a commandeering of the debate on boys' education and a thorough talking down over the extent of the crisis. If a crisis of achievement does exist, it is more likely found within issues of race and class. Martino and Kehler (2006) urged that "interrogation of the intersecting factors of class, race, ethnicity and sexuality is needed, specifically in terms of their impact on groups of boys and men that differ significantly from dominant white males" (p. 125). If only these arguments could reach the mainstream.

An important goal for recapturing the boys' debate is to continue work on non-hegemonic masculinities in schools. Much of this center on understanding how alternative masculinities are "negotiated" in a school environment that enforces a dominant and repressive form of boyhood (Dalley-Trim, 2007; Jackson, 2003; O'Donoghue, 2007; Renold, 2004). "The cultural formation of young men's identities generates specific masculine subjectivities that cannot be reduced to a singular notion of maleness" (Haywood, Popoviciu, & Mac an Ghaill, 2005, p. 204). Thus, it is important to the male teacher debate to understand how formative school experiences influence the choice to teach, which is a contestable form of adult masculinity. Teachers and school staff are furthermore essential to student achievement and to their understanding of the limitations of single definitions of masculinity and femininity (Martino et al., 2004; Mills, 2000). It is only proper then to consider how individuals, who spend considerable amounts of time with children, second only to parents or immediate family, can affect how tenets of hegemonic masculinity form. As suggested by Mills and Keddie (2007), the development of a curriculum or pedagogy to combat gender bias in schools could eventually lead to the shedding of damaging forms of masculinity and an embrace of social justice along gender lines.

Linking Multiple Masculinities

Another important challenge posed by the progressive literature is forging linkages between newer work on gender and masculinity to the century old debate on both male teachers and the fear of the "feminization" of school environments. Progressive work on male teachers especially reinforces the connection that working with children is a non-hegemonic form of masculinity challenging conventional gender norms (Carrington, 2002; DeCorse & Vogtle, 1997; Frank & Martino, 2006; Jamison, 2000; Mills et al., 2008; Skelton, 2003; Smedley, 2007; Warren, 2003). One could make a sterile psychological argument here: working in a job that challenges cultural norms could cause a substantial amount of stress due to gender role conflict. Fortunately, in a novel contribution to the male teacher issue, Wolfram, Mohr, & Borchert (2009) observed that male primary teachers "reported moderate levels of anxiety, depression, emotional irritation, and gender-role conflict," yet their presence in a female-dominated profession did not lead to lowered work satisfaction. In fact, high femininity ascriptions were more likely to produce work-related dissatisfaction.

A discourse of teaching masculinity as a contestable form is a progressive alternative to that of male teachers modeling hallmarks real masculinity for young children. Mills (2004) took it one step further by arguing that a critical examination of the various justifications for male teachers can open up larger conversations about misogyny and homophobia as Mills points out that there "is a general silence about such issues in education" (p. 35). Linking the debate on male teachers to recent work on multiple masculinities forces accountability to larger social phenomena that contributes to the gender disparities in teaching. Linkages also label crisis commentary about male teachers appropriately as "anxiety about the status of masculinity in times of a feminist backlash" and a "repudiation of the feminine" by bashing women's work (Martino, 2008, p. 218). Rifts between dominant and subordinated masculinities even persist within the teaching profession, as noted in the "disciplining of John," a male primary school teacher who did not conform to populist tropes of man as disciplinarian and sports fan (Martino, 2008). Usurpation of the gendered agenda is ultimately about privilege: attention shifted to boys and the need to mentor them by men are subtle nudges to reassert prior entitlements. Progressive challenges endeavor to justify male teachers as a sign of shifting cultural conditions and not as paragons of traditional norms.

Productive Pedagogies

Progressive challenges to crisis discourse regarding male teachers is largely dominated by authors such as Raewyn Connell, Rebecca Francis, Robert Lingard, Wayne Martino, Martin Mills, and Christine Skelton who hail from Australia, Canada, and the United Kingdom. This final note, however, on schools as progressive battle-grounds belongs to Amanda Keddie, a scholar from the University of Queensland. It does not seem customary to pay homage to a specific researcher. Keddie's research, however, on actively promoting gender justice in schools deserves an explicit reference because it demonstrates a radicalization of the values and principles of the previous authors' ideas.

In its most elemental form, Keddie (2006) argued for a school environment "informed by key feminist understandings of masculinity" and for teachers to develop "a critical reflective and transformative approach that seeks to challenge and rework (rather than normalize and reinscribe) boys' narrow constructions of gender" (p. 111). Although much of her work focuses on boys' education, Keddie advocated overall for the development of "critical literacy" to transform and disrupt "narrow ways of being male and female" (2008, p. 580). Stripping the power from prevailing gender norms for men and boys is especially relevant to the male teacher issue. Conventional masculinity prohibits participation in women's work. But the impetus for change must also reach women and girls because they are for now teachers and the primary caregivers. Keddie and Mills (2009) together profiled examples of "trans-formative pedagogies" in various Australian primary and secondary schools. They conclude that "blindly adopting boy-friendly strategies will compound gender in-justices currently perpetuated in many schools" (p. 41). Moreover, the "valorization" of dominant masculinity buried within mainstream calls for male teachers reify the exact dim values limiting their participation.

As a final note, Keddie repeatedly advocated for a variation of a "productive pedagogies" framework, retooled from its initial function, to promote gender justice in schools that:

> draws on feminist principles to focus on valuing difference and diversity provides a platform for teachers to begin articulating affirmative "ways of being" with boys and, within this framework, to begin questioning and challenging rather than reinscribing the narrow or dominant versions of gender and hierar-chical constructions of masculinity that constrain boys' (and girls') academic and social outcomes. (2006, p. 102).

27

The productive pedagogies model was originally devised and promoted by The State of Queensland, Australia in 2001 to improve the educational outcomes of boys. The framework consists of four central themes, each with a number of subthemes and reflective questions: intellectual quality, connectedness, supportive classroom environment, and recognition of difference. Productive pedagogies is hailed as a model that draws attention to race, class, gender, and other social factors as "markers" of achievement and encourages dialogue between teachers and students on such issues (Hayes, Lingard, & Mills, 2000). As an alternative to simplistic boy-friendly strategies, Mills and Keddie (2007) argued that "the productive pedagogies framework refuses to treat boys who are struggling with school as deficit, whilst at the same time encouraging all boys to trouble those aspects of masculinity which are damaging to them and to others" (p. 350). This pedagogical model is certainly not the solution to our problems and, to my knowledge, no evaluations of its performance in Australian classrooms are available. Nevertheless, this model and Keddie's work exemplify the current effort and future possibilities of the struggle to radicalize progressive values and gender justice in schools.

Conclusion

At a conference where I was discussing some of my research on men in education, I was asked a rather difficult question: do male teachers make any special contribution in schools? I paused for a moment and answered truthfully that they do not. At first, I felt like all of my experiences as a male elementary teacher and the advocacy work I have done on their behalf suddenly withered away. How could I make such a statement and still claim that their relative absence from the classroom is a problem? After a thorough bit of reflection, I knew deep down that the argument that male teachers make special contributions to schools only because of their gender is still part of the problem. The language of gendered divisions, of separate men's and women's roles, is subtle and serious. As long as we embrace the idea that on some general level an inclusion of men in schools would achieve a gendered balance, then we are not far from extrapolating that to the division of men's and women's work.

I marvel on occasion at how gendered our world actually is for children. From an early age, they are inundated with preferences, activities, and colors that they should prefer because of their biological sex. Each passing year yields new information on gender and sexuality, so much complicated information that I feel we should put these traditional assumptions to rest. Those that advocate for more male teachers in the United States must come to the realization that any and all rhetoric based on differences between genders and the separation of their roles are what fundamentally cause the paucity of men in teaching. The education of children has a long tradition of being assigned as women's work; moreover, men and boys have long been told that feminine activities must be avoided at all costs. Granted, the limitations are weakening, yet they still run strong and they run very deep. With the feminist gains over the last few decades, sexist, homophobic, and misogynist biases retreated in many cases to the subtle and almost indiscernible. But they are still there, nonetheless.

Early childhood and elementary educators are in an enviable position, at least to some. Of all the competing influences for children's attentions, teachers are left with a reasonable amount of influence on young people. What are educators to do with this power? Is it important to leave assumptions untested and continue with business as usual? Or, is it time to cease cursing the dark and make a difference? Formal schooling as an institution leaves an indelible mark on the lives of children and young adults. The institution, however, is deeply marred by unquestioned traditions, notably its ongoing and condoned division of labor.

Sugg (1978) controversially argued that "the feminization of teachers was an effectual solution to American ambivalence about education" (p. 109). Is that possible? Are we so ambivalent about who teaches our children that it is acceptable to leave the male teacher problem unsolved? Perhaps it is possible for reformers to demand simultaneously that the profession include not only quality teachers but also those that adequately represent the population it serves. The bulk of this responsibility does belong to educators who are at present molding and shaping the future possibilities of children. Whether those include men in care giving roles, it is up to those who currently raise and model acceptable behavior for children to decide.

REFERENCES

Anderson, K. J., & Accomando, C. (2002). 'Real' boys? Manufacturing masculinity and erasing privilege in popular books on raising boys. *Feminism Psychology, 19*, 491–516.

Bastick, T. (2000). Why teacher trainees choose the teaching profession: Comparing trainees in metropolitan and developing countries. *International Review of Education, 46*(3/4), 343–349.

Bricheno, P., & Thornton, M. (2007). Role model, hero or champion? Children's views concerning role models. *Educational Research, 49*(4), 383–396,

Bureau of Labor Statistics. (2007). *Employed persons by detailed occupation, sex, race, and Hispanic or Latino ethnicity, 2007*. Retrieved from Bureau of Labor Statistics Web site: http://www.bls.gov/

Carrington, B. (2002). A quintessentially feminine domain? Student teachers' constructions of primary teaching as a career. *Educational Studies, 28*(3), 287–303.

Carrington, B., Tymms, P., & Merrell, C. (2005). *Role models, school improvement and the "gender gap"—Do men bring out the best in boys and women the best in girls?* EARLI 2005 conference. University of Nicosia.

Connell, R. W. (1988). *Gender and power: Society, the person, and sexual politics.* Stanford, CA: Stanford University Press.

Connell, R. W. (1995). *Masculinities.* Berkeley, CA: University of California Press.

Coulter, R. P., & McNay, M. (1993). Exploring men's experiences as elementary school teachers. *Canadian Journal of Education, 18*(4), 398–413.

Cushman, P. (2005). Let's hear if from the males: Issues facing male primary school teachers. *Teaching and Teacher Education, 21*, 227–240.

Dalley-Trim, L. (2007). 'The boys' present... Hegemonic masculinity: A performance of multiple acts. *Gender & Education, 19*(2), 199–217.

DeCorse, C. J., & Vogtle, S. (1997). In a complex voice: The contradictions of male elementary teachers' career choice and professional identity. *Journal of Teacher Education, 48*, 37–46.

Driessen, G. (2007). The feminization of primary education: Effects of teachers' sex on pupil achievement, attitudes and behavior. *Review of Education, 53*, 183–203.

Drudy, S., Martin, M., Woods, M., & O'Flynn, J. (2005). *Men in the classroom: Gender imbalances in teaching.* London: Routledge.

Foster, T., & Newman, E. (2005). Just a knock back? Identity bruising on the route to becoming a male primary school teacher. *Teachers and Teaching: theory and practice, 11*(4), 341–358.

Francis, B., & Skelton, C. (2001). Men teachers and the construction of heterosexual masculinity in the classroom. *Sex Education, 1*(1), 9–21.

Francis, B., & Skelton, C. (2005). *Reassessing gender and achievement: Questioning contemporary key debates*. New York: Routledge.

Francis, B., Skelton, C., Carrington, B., Hutchings, M., & Read, B. (2008). A prefect match? Pupils' and teachers' views of the impact of matching educators and learners by gender. *Research Papers in Education, 23*(1), 21–36.

Frank, B., & Martino, W. (2006). The tyranny of surveillance: Male teachers and the policing of masculinities in a single sex school. *Gender and Education, 18*(1), 17–33.

Gaskell, J., & Mullen, A. (2006). Women in teaching: Participation, power and possibility. In C. Skelton, B. Francis, & L. Smulyan (Eds.), *The SAGE handbook of gender and education* (pp. 453–468). Thousand Oaks: SAGE Publications.

Gold, D., & Reis, M. (1982). Male teacher effects on young children: A theoretical and empirical consideration. *Sex Roles, 8*(5), 493–513.

Goodman, J. (1987). Masculinity, feminism, and the male elementary school teacher: A case study of preservice teachers' perspectives. *Journal of Curriculum Theorizing, 7*(2), 30–55.

Goodman, J., & Kelly, T. (1988). Out of the mainstream: Issues confronting the male profeminist elementary school teacher. *Interchange, 19*(2), 1–14.

Gorard, S., Rees, G., & Salisbury, J. (1999). Reappraising the apparent underachievement of boys at school. *Gender and Education, 11*(4), 441–454.

Gutmann, A. (1987). *Democratic education*. Princeton, NJ: Princeton University Press.

Hansen, P., & Mulholland, J. A. (2005). Caring and elementary teaching: The concerns of male beginning teachers. *Journal of Teacher Education, 56*, 119–131.

Hayes, D., Lingard, B., & Mills, M. (2000). Productive pedagogies. *Education Links*, 10–13.

Haywood, C., Popoviciu, L., & Mac an Ghaill, M. (2005). Fulmination and schooling: Re-masculinisation, gendered reflexivity and boyness. *Irish Journal of Sociology, 14*(2), 193–212.

Hoff-Summers, C. (2000). *The war against boys*. New York: Simon & Schuster.

Jackson, C. (2003). Motives for "Laddishness" at school: fear of failure and fear of the 'feminine.' *British Educational Research Journal, 29*(4), 583–598.

Jamison, J. (2000). Negotiating otherness: A male early childhood educator's gender positioning. *International Journal of Early Years Education, 8*(2), 129–139.

Keddie, A. (2006). Pedagogies and critical reflection: Key understandings for transformative gender justice. *Gender & Education, 18*(1), 99–114.

Keddie, A. (2008). Gender Justice and the English citizenship curriculum: A consideration of Post-September 11 national imperatives and issues of "Britishness." *International Journal of Educational Reform, 17*(1), 3–18.

Keddie, A., & Mills, M. (2009). Disrupting masculinised spaces: Teachers working for gender justice. *Research Papers in Education, 24*(1), 29–43.

King, J. R. (1998). *Uncommon caring: Learning from men who teach young children*. New York: Teachers College Press.

Lahelma, E. (2000). Lack of male teachers: A problem for students or teachers? *Pedagogy, Culture and Society, 8*(2), 173–186.

Lewis, E., Butcher, J., & Donnan, P. (2006). *Men in primary teaching: An endangered species?* Retrieved March 25, 2006, from http://www.aare.edu.au/99pap/but99238.htm

Mac an Ghaill, M. (1996). 'What about the boys?': Schooling, class, and crisis masculinity. *The Editorial Board of the Sociological Review*, 381–397.

Maloutas, M. P. (2006). *The gender of democracy*. New York: Routledge.

Martino, W., Lingard, B., & Mills, M. (2004). Issues in boys' education: A question of teacher threshold knowledges? *Gender and Education, 16*(4), 435–454.

Martino, W., & Kehler, M. (2006). Male teachers and the "boy problem": An issue of recuperative masculinity politics. *McGill Journal of Education, 41*(2), 113–131.

Martino, W. J. (2008). Male teachers as role models: Addressing issues of masculinity, pedagogy and the re-masculinization of schooling. *Curriculum Inquiry, 38*(2), 189–223.

Mead, S. (2006). *The evidence suggests otherwise: The truth about boys and girls*. Washington, DC: Education Sector.

Mills, M. (2000). Issues in implementing boys' programme in schools: Male teachers and empowerment. *Gender and Education, 12*(2), 221–238.

Mills, M. (2004). Male teachers, homophobia, misogyny, and teacher education. *Teaching Education, 15*(1), 27–39.

Mills, M., Martino, W. & Lingard, B. (2004). Attracting, recruiting, and retaining male teachers: Policy issues in the male teacher debate. *British Journal of Sociology of Education, 25*(3), 355–369.

Mills, M., & Keddie, A. (2007). Teaching boys and gender justice. *International Journal of Inclusive Education, 11*(3), 335–354.

Mills, M., & Lingard, B. (2007). Pedagogies making a difference: Of social justice and inclusion. *International Journal of Inclusive Education, 11*(3), 233–244.

Mills, M., Haase, M., & Charlton, E. (2008). Being the 'right' kind of male teacher: The disciplining of John. *Pedagogy, Culture and Society, 16*(1), 71–84.

Montecinos, C., & Nielson, L. (2004). Male elementary pre-service teachers' gendering of teaching. *Multicultural Perspectives, 6*(2), 3–9.

National Education Association. (2007). *Rankings and estimates of the states 2006 and estimates of school statistics 2007*. Retrieved January 1, 2009, from http://www.nea.org/edstats

O'Donoghue, D. O. (2007). 'James always hangs out here': Making space for place in studying masculinities at school. *Visual Studies, 22*(1), 62–71.

Paradise, L. V., & Wall, S. M. (1986). Children's perceptions of male and female principals and teachers. *Sex Roles, 14*(1/2), 1–7.

Renold, E. (2004). 'Other' boys: Negotiating non-hegemonic masculinities in the primary school. *Gender and Education, 16*(2), 247–266.

Roulston, K., & Mills, M. (2000). Male teachers in feminized teaching areas: Marching to the beat of the men's movement drums? *Oxford Review of Education, 26*(2), 221–237.

Sargent, P. (2001). *Real Men or real teachers: Contradictions in the lives of men elementary school teachers*. Harriman: Men's Studies Press.

Sax, L. (2008). *Boys adrift: The five factors driving the growing epidemic of unmotivated boys and underachieving young men*. New York: Basic Books.

Skelton, C. (2003). Male primary teachers and perceptions of masculinity. *Educational Review, 55*(2), 195–209.

Smedley, S., & Pepperell, S. (2000). No man's land: Caring and male student primary teachers. *Teachers and Teaching: theory and practice, 6*(3), 259–277.

Smedley, S. (2007). Learning to be a primary school teacher: Reading one man's story. *Gender and Education, 19*(3), 369–385.

Sugg, R. S., Jr. (1978). *Motherteacher: The feminization of American education*. Charlottesville, VA: University Press of Virginia.

Sumison, J. (1999). Critical reflections on the experiences of a male early childhood worker. *Gender and Education, 11*(4), 455–468.

Titus, J. J. (2004). Boy trouble: Rhetorical framing of boys' underachievement. *Discourse: Studies in the cultural politics of education, 25*(2), 145–169.

Tsouroufli, M. (2002). Gender and teachers' practice in a secondary school in Greece. *Gender and Education, 14*(2), 135–147.

Tyre, P. (2008). *The trouble with boys: A surprising report card on our sons, their problems at school, and what parents and educators must do*. New York: Crown Publishers.

UNESCO. (2008). *United Nations educational, scientific and cultural organization world education indicators percentage of female teachers in the school years 2004–2005.* Retrieved from UNESCO National Institute for Statistics Web site: http://www.uis.unesco.org

Warren, S. (2003). Is that an action man in there? Masculinity as an imaginative act of self-creation. *Discourse: Studies in the cultural politics of education, 24*(1), 3–18.

Weaver-Hightower, M. (2003). The "boy turn" in research on gender and education. *Review of Educational Research, 73*(4), 471–498.

Wolfram, H., Mohr, G., & Borchert, J. (2009). Gender role self-concept, gender-role conflict, and well-being in male primary school teachers. *Sex Roles, 60,* 114–127.

SCOTT A. MORRISON

4. THE GIFT

A Charge to Keep I Have

I remember sitting on the couch in the activity room, one of the few places where an air conditioner provided a cool respite from the July heat. In the background, I heard the melodic hum of soft voices and occasional bursts of high-pitched laughter as girls sang songs to the rhythm of their slapping hands. Boys were scattered around a dark green table chasing a ping-pong ball that hit the floor more often that it hit the paddles. A half-dozen nine- and ten-year-olds sat comfortably near me and a few other counselors; the kids listened attentively to our tall tales with wide-eyed wonder. The festive air was sweet medicine for us all. That afternoon is quite clear to me although it occurred about twenty years ago. The smiles, the innocence, and the shared delight were poignant—almost palpable—even to a naïve fifteen-year-old. What started as a means to interrupt the monotony of summer, volunteering for a week as a junior counselor at a local Christian camp, turned into something more. The joy of being in the presence of children resonated with me, and soon after I gained a desire to continue working with children. Teaching had become my *calling*.

When others discovered my intentions, they eagerly offered commentary. In some cases, jokes were made about paltry pay and lax summer vacations. More often than not, though, affirmations gushed. "We need more men in the classroom," I would hear. "Kids need male role models," was another enthusiastic refrain. As a teenager, I did not grasp the totality of such remarks. I just took every word as a compliment and felt emboldened to continue. I somehow knew that teaching young children was more or less a feminized profession, yet I did not let that puzzlement detract me. In fact, part of me pressed on simply out of spite. I relished taking the unbeaten path, at times anyway. My green Chuck Taylors with yellow laces were legendary in middle school, so I channeled my harmless teenage rebellion toward the unconventional yet again. But for me, and for others in my community, there was also a divine element involved. Reared in church, God infused virtually all aspects of life. If I had indeed heard the voice of the Creator, then my decision was less of a career move and more of a spiritual mission. Framing my longing to work with children as a religious affair simplified the matter. God spoke, and I obeyed. I was not pursing a profession as much as surrendering to the will of the Almighty. And this made perfect sense at the time.

I would be lying, though, if I did not admit that the admiration of others—of the children I worked with and of the adults who showered me with praise—was the

W.Watson and C.S.Woods (eds), Go Where You Belong:
Cultural Workers in the Lives of Children, Families, and Communities, 33–38.
© 2011 Sense Publishers. All rights reserved.

primary god I served. Like most teenagers, I wrestled with self-esteem and social acceptance; my thin shell of confidence more often than not masked doubt and insecurity. I liked being accepted, and the vocational niche I embodied—a young man participating in the lives of children—provided me with direction, stability, and identity. And that proved quite powerful.

To a certain degree, family history was a similar important influence. My father is a teacher, and my grandmother was, too, though neither professionally. Which is why it took me a while to figure out that teaching is a family tradition. My father and grandmother honed their skills on Sunday mornings at church. With supernatural inspiration, they synthesized and analyzed Biblical tales in a manner quite captivating and clear. When my grandmother passed away unexpectedly, I traveled halfway across the country to attend her funeral. Those who spoke of her life and legacy never failed to mention her *gift*. To hear others describe my grandmother as transformative caused me to reflect on the course my life should take and what I wished others would say about me after I depart. Such reflection touched me profoundly. From that point forward, I adopted another word to describe my choice to become a teacher. Not only did I hear a *calling*, but I also inherited a *gift*. My destiny was clear; my path was fully illuminated.

While in college, I took advantage of various opportunities to gain experience, build my resume, and have fun with children. This initially included coaching a boys' soccer team for the local parks and recreation department, which in turn led to other coaching opportunities for several years to come. On the pitch is where I experimented with pedagogy and learned how to effectively manage over a dozen young bodies for an hour or two. I can blame the culture of sports or the follies of youth, but there were some bumps in the road, too. My face still blushes when I recollect some of my more egregious errors: poor word choices in the heat of frustration; weak (or even non-existent) relationships with the parents of players; indifference to socio-economic divisions; and an unhealthy emphasis on winning.

With gentle and humbling guidance from gracious adults, I learned from the lapses. On the one hand, I look back upon those soccer practices as indispensible teacher training. On the other hand, coaching fourth- and fifth-graders eager to run and play is somewhat different from teaching thirty pre-teens about Socrates and Ancient Greece. After four years in training, I emerged as a promising teacher that did not bat an eye at the thought of keeping a classroom full of kids occupied— *entertained*, even—for an entire day. Years on the sideline shouting instructions and praise prepared me to project my voice and command a room; short attention spans were commonplace, so I knew how to organize and adjust my plans accordingly. Moving into the classroom was thus a natural and logical progression.

My experiences and university degree did indeed groom me in large part for life as a teacher. I could generate student interest with a lead question or activity; integrate technology, music, and art. I also used cooperative groups in such a way that made learning more social and less cumbersome. But as a young man in my early twenties at a small elementary school in a tight-knit town, there were numerous unexpected struggles. In the following paragraphs, I highlight four.

First, I did little to sufficiently nurture my students. Even though I knew that teachers should attend to the *whole* child, I typically focused solely on the intellect. I prioritized learning objectives and expected students to adhere to my plans diligently. This does not suggest a dictatorial style, a lack of compassion, or even strict discipline on my part. In fact, my loose and creative approach unsettled other teachers with whom I worked. My mistake was limiting my interaction with students to the academic; I implicitly required them to check their lives at the door and not let family conflicts, the latest gossip, or their worries and fears disrupt the learning process. The roots of this behavior are complicated. My own socialization—media influences, experiences with male teachers and coaches throughout my schooling, my relationship with my father and uncles—contributed to the construction of my image both as *man* and *ideal teacher*. Ironically, my attention to the cognitive was positively affirmed. No administrators or parents faulted me for having high academic expectations and maximizing time-on-task.

But in hindsight I see more clearly where I dropped the ball and failed to lend a nurturing hand. For example, I did not know how to respond to the news that Heather's parents had split rather suddenly—her father taking off with another woman and fleeing to another state—so I remained silent. I conveniently down-played Tiffany's degenerative muscle condition that ultimately put her in a wheel-chair. Likewise, Joseph's arthritic hip required two surgeries, yet I felt that keeping track of the work he missed was my only responsibility. I knew that Billy's father was an alcoholic and that his sister was undergoing treatment for a variety of serious illnesses, but I only recall telling him to sit still, get his act together, and study more. Tsing spoke no English; I figured he would learn the language just by being there. And when Brooke came to school even during chemotherapy, my arms did not reach out once for a hug. Such memories are painful, and these are just the more obvious ones. There were hundreds of other minor incidences, no doubt. As a pre-service teacher in college, I remember being given two specific pieces of advice. First, do not be a friend to the students. To do so is to compromise your authority and increase your chances of losing control of student behavior. Second, because you are a male, do not touch the students under any circumstances. One misplaced hand or one misinterpreted act of kindness could cost you your job and even your career. While there is certainly some truth to that counsel, I regret not doing more to nurture deeper and more caring relationships with my students—especially those most in need.

Second, though I was aware that most teachers of young children are female—from my own experiences in school and even the composition of my undergraduate program—I was not very comfortable working with middle-aged women. The first two years were especially awkward. I remember attending team and faculty meetings at the beginning of the school year, hoping to locate another male with whom I could connect. To be sure, there were a few men in the school, but they were much older than me and had children of their own; we lived in different worlds. Consequently, I was rather lonely. I basically shut my door—both literally and figuratively—because there was no one within the school with whom I could easily relate.

Granted, over the years I eventually developed strong relationships with my colleagues; however, the process was long and slow.

During my first year, I was the only male on a six-teacher team, and the youngest female teacher was at least ten years my senior. The women were extremely nice, but I quickly picked up that we shared more differences than our gender. I was questioning the faith of my youth; two of my co-workers were married to pastors. I was experimenting with alternative pedagogy; they basically stuck to traditional methods. I encouraged vibrant participation from my students; they regularly reminded me to keep the "noise" down so their students could concentrate. Given the context, I hesitated to voice my own opinions during our planning meetings, which were intended, ironically, to foster unity and collaboration. I was outnumbered. My mentor was the same age as my own mother. Who was I to question, advice, or criticize? My solution? Smile, nod and be quiet.

Fortunately, during my third year of teaching another young man, Will, was hired to teach third grade. Given my habit of reclusive behavior, it took me a while to extend a hand of friendship. But by the end of that year we had become close friends. That same year, Rob was hired as an interim fifth grade teacher. We now numbered three. Finally, I had colleagues with whom I identified. We swapped stories; we vented frustrations; we laughed at the ironies and idiosyncrasies of our work. The five years we spent in the same school were priceless and had quite an effect on my growth as a teacher. The male camaraderie aided my development. Being comfortable led me to embrace my unique presence in the school.

Third, despite my experience working with the parents of the players I coached, I had trouble relating to the issues and concerns of the parents of my students. I had no children of my own, so my ideas about child rearing were raw and untested. There were two instances that occurred my first year teaching that challenged my ability to empathize and counsel. On the first day of school a sea of emotions was swirling inside of me. Adrenaline compensated for a significant lack of sleep. I had worked tirelessly for three straight days, holed up in my classroom well past midnight each night in order to plan, photocopy, staple, organize, clean, and rehearse. Silvia's mother greeted me at the door and kindly introduced herself. After a few short exchanges, she leaned in closer to my ear and quietly said: "And just so you know, Silvia recently stared her period. I've given her what she needs, and I think she'll be all right, but just in case I thought you should know." I nodded my head and thanked her for sharing this information, but inside I was not so calm. *Did I just hear what I think I heard? Which one is Silvia? What do I know about menstruation? Why did she tell me this?* Silvia was fine that day and every other. I, however, was given a jolt of reality before the first bell had even sounded.

Nine weeks later provided more opportunities to learn about the unexpected. The occasion? Parent-teacher conferences. My mentor recommended I call every parent to set up a time; this method worked for her, and since I could not think of an alternative I followed her lead. I was nervous to say the least. I stared at the phone reluctantly before dialing each number, feeling vulnerable and uncomfortable. I eventually contacted them all—without a hitch—and managed to schedule everyone for a 15-minute session. The most memorable was one of the last.

Mark's mother was petite and attractive; her long dark hair and stylish clothes set her apart. I explained that her son was doing well for the most part, but that he was struggling a little here and there. Attempting to end on a positive note, I complimented her son's manners and generous spirit. Just when I thought we were about to conclude she said, "There is something about Mark that I am concerned about." I trained my eyes on her, unsure of what she might say. "Lately he has been secretly going through my underwear drawer and playing with my lingerie." After three beats of awkward silence, she continued, "Do you know anything about this kind of behavior?" I had no idea what to say. My mind could barely process the words; I could feel my face redden by the second. Grasping for an answer, I managed, "I am not sure what to make of it, to be honest. Mark does not display particularly unusual behavior at school. Perhaps this is just a phase. Have you spoken with him about it?" She had not done so yet and was not sure if she should. "Since his father and I are divorced," she went on, "Mark does not have a man in his life to talk to about these things." I nodded and let several more beats of silence pass. Befuddled, I redirected the conversation back to his school performance. A few minutes later she walked out the door, high heels clicking loudly down the hallway. I returned to my desk, took a deep breath, and put my face in my hands.

Fourth, I emphasized heteronormativity. In other words, I communicated to my students that people fall into only one of two distinct and complementary sexes with each having certain natural roles in life. By doing so, I stigmatized and marginalized alternative forms of sexuality and gender. My tactics were slight, and my chief concern in most cases was classroom management and not social commentary. For instance, every year I had boys in my classroom who were energetic and tactile, and they touched each other frequently—from high-fives and handshakes to head-locks and hallway wrestling matches. My primary recourse for discouraging such distracting (and sometimes dangerous or intimidating) behavior was to sexualize the physical contact and ostracize the students. "I know you guys like to touch each other," I would say, "but you need to save that until after school." This comment usually elicited giggles from classmates to the dismay of the perpetrators. Sometimes I piled on more: "If you boys need to talk to the counselor, I can walk down the hall and see if she is available."

Luckily, a student had the audacity to challenge me on this practice. Instead of approaching me, though, he went straight to my superior. One afternoon the principal beckoned me to his office during my planning period. The stern look on his face set my heart racing. He quickly proceeded to recount his conversation with one of my students—the same student I had reprimanded earlier that day for continuously poking a less popular classmate—and then inform me that my words were out of line, that embarrassing students not an effective means of discipline, and that the effects of my language send messages to other students that are equally harmful. I sheepishly nodded in agreement, yet it took a while for his message to hit home. Heteronormativity was not a word in my vocabulary at that point—and it probably was not in my principal's either—but he had enough sense to recognize that which I did not.

After eleven years in the classroom, I have regrettably forgotten more than I have remembered. Former students like to reminisce with me about our lives together, and sometimes the stories they tell are quite different from mine. Often I am asked if I recall certain incidents, and when I do not, the story is enthusiastically retold. We tend to remember outliers, experiences that defy expectations. Witty comments, activities that took us outside, and humorous exchanges endure in our collective memories. For example, students joyfully recollect the practical joke I played on the teacher across the hall; I suspended her reading glasses from the ceiling during her lunch period, and her students stifled laughter as she searched the room frantically to find them. On another occasion, I allowed my students to experiment with *Mentos* and 2-liter bottles of Diet Coke—YouTube videos provided the idea and motivation. I regularly made appearances in the gymnasium on Fridays to participate in free play; 9-square games, ultimate, and half-court basketball allowed us to relate on a different level and build unique memories around sport and competition. The year I decided to build an organic garden with my students on school grounds is especially unforgettable. We spent hours outside together getting sweaty and dirty, and in the end we literally tasted the fruit of our labor. My students and I carry those moments with us, and reflecting on those sweet times reminds me why I enjoy participating in the lives of children so much.

Despite some early struggles, I am proud of what I have accomplished so far in my teaching career. Recounting the hurdles I had to overcome, which I hope are instructive, tells only part of the story. In fact, I hesitate mentioning the mistakes for fear of painting too negative a picture. This is simply a selective snapshot intended to illuminate that which others must beware. If ever I am tempted to wallow in the dissatisfactions of my work, I simply call to mind a special memory that reorients my pessimism. One of my favorites occurred during my second year in the classroom. On a warm June morning, I asked my students to sit on the floor in a circle. Summer vacation commenced the next day, and I needed to express my thanks and love for time well spent. The setting was perfect. Sunlight streamed through the window and illuminated our faces. The gleam in their eyes reflected passion for life and a yearning for freedom. I gathered several sheets of paper from my desk and sat amongst them. Their chatter quieted. Clearing my throat, I started reading the poem I had written for them just days before. I recited the lines slowly, letting them absorb each syllable. That they were calm and attentive is testament to the special bond we shared. I had chosen this method to honor them, to communicate my appreciation for their presence in my life. When I finished reading, the tears and the laughter marked a fitting conclusion.

Little did I know what I was committing myself to as a fifteen-year-old. I certainly have no regrets. Children benefit from having men in their lives. In my own experience, the piles of hand-written thank-you notes I have received, and the warm exchanges with students and their parents, bear incredible witness.

PATRICK LEWIS

5. FEELING SPECIAL AND FEELING LOUSY

My teaching stories are, to borrow from Grumet (1991), "not extraordinary." I tell them at the risk of offending scholarly sensibilities but these are the stories I know and carry with me. As Grumet points out, when these stories "are omitted from our scholarship, when we look elsewhere, anywhere, for our sources, our reasons and motives, we perpetuate and exaggerate our exile. We deny…and in that denial we cut the ground right out from under us" (pp. 83–84).

Tanja had come to my class 4 months ago. Before her arrival, I had met with the principal, the special education teacher, and the district psychologist. They all had read the great tomes of information about Tanja and her previous experiences with the public education system and social services. The meeting was set to discuss her placement at the little school of one hundred K-8 students. I knew ahead of time that they wanted her placed in my grade 1-2 class even though she was 9 years old because I was the only classroom teacher asked to the meeting. I had listened to their reasons and then expressed my concerns and arranged for the necessary classroom support. She would arrive in a week.

Tanja, according to the running narrative of her file, had a plethora of emotional, psychological, and learning problems that plagued her in such a short early age. The most recent addition to her file was that she had Tourette syndrome. I had read the medical fact sheet in her file, describing the various symptoms, traits, characteristics, and aspects of this neurological disorder: the tendency to make loud noises with the expulsion of air from the mouth; involuntary twitching, tics and vocalizations; and compulsive utterance of obscenities. Added to these behaviors were her occasional outbursts of angry, aggressive, and sometimes violent actions. I had wondered just how this child would make out in my class and how the class would make out with her.

The file also had information about the medication the child was taking in order to try and minimize the effects of the syndrome on her learning as well as other medication to help focus her attention. Essentially, she took a heavy dose of depressants that had the side effect of causing severe depression and, subsequently, she was given some antidepressants to offset the side effect of the former. Each morning as school began her heavy drug intake was abundantly apparent when one looked into Tanja's eyes.

After three months of trying to have Tanja remain in class all day with the rest of the children, it had become clear this would not work for me, Tanja, her support aid, or the rest of the children. Mrs. Hill, and the principal, and I decided that each

W.Watson and C.S.Woods (eds), Go Where You Belong:
Cultural Workers in the Lives of Children, Families, and Communities, 39–45.
© *2011 Sense Publishers. All rights reserved.*

afternoon after the lunch break Tanja would work for the first hour with Mrs. Hill in the learning assistance room. She would then return to class for the remainder of the day. We tried this for the last several weeks with varying degrees of success.

Nevertheless, it usually helped center her energy, which in turn reduced the number of times she would have angry, and sometimes, violent outbursts accompanied by the long tirade of obscenities. The litany of obscenities seemed to be the only trait of Tourette syndrome she ever demonstrated at school; it would be learned later, that Tanja did not in fact have Tourette syndrome. Tanja didn't always want to leave the class and sometimes had to be persuaded, encouraged, or both.

On one such occasion, Tanja was determined not to go with Mrs. Hill or anyone else. At one o'clock all the children in my class were busy settling down with a variety of reading material for the daily ritual of silent reading. That is, all the children were doing this, except Tanja. She was standing by me with her lower lip and chin jutting out in an effort to demonstrate her displeasure and resolve not to go with Mrs. Hill today. I was standing by the classroom doorway, which was right next to a closet doorway in the room. Mrs. Hill had just walked in, and I was handing her some of the learning materials I wanted her to use with Tanja. I also explained what she might try working on with Tanja. As I did this, Tanja began to stamp her foot decisively upon the floor screeching, through clenched teeth, "I'm not going! I'm not going!"

I tried to ignore her and proceeded to continue detailing instructions to Mrs. Hill. It was becoming increasingly obvious to me that Mrs. Hill was finding it difficult to listen to what I was saying, as Tanja became louder and more determined in her objections.

Tanja, at that point, decided that stamping and screaming were insufficient. She rushed at me brandishing her newly sharpened pencil and attempting to stab me with it. I was pushed back against the small bit of wall between the two doorways and tried to stop her thrust, but not before the pencil tore through my shirt and stung the flesh below my right shoulder. Tanja was tall and very strong. Her strength seemed to increase dramatically when she became angry. Mrs. Hill decided that the best thing to do would be to take two steps back and declare, "Tanja that behavior is completely unacceptable. You let go of Mr. Lewis right now!"

Tanja did not let me go. However, I took a firm grip on Tanja and pushed her arms down, moving her back several steps while controlling a stronger and deeper urge to respond to her attack in a less than civilized way. Then, I continued explaining what Mrs. Hill and Tanja would be working on. Tanja could not bear it. She was determined to win the day. She lunged at me and pushed me backward into the closet and slammed the door shut, putting all her weight and considerable strength against it while holding the doorknob tightly. I pulled myself slowly out of the shelving I had fallen into and tried to open the door. Tanja held fast, resisting my efforts.

I could hear Mrs. Hill demanding, "Let Mr. Lewis out immediately!" She indicated to Tanja that if she did not do so, she would have to face dire consequences for her actions. She then threatened to go and get the principal. Mrs. Hill's voice was faint, and I could only assume she had taken a few more steps toward the hall door to ensure a hasty escape if Tanja were to turn her attention toward her. The threat of the principal, like always, had no affect on Tanja. I implored Tanja, in a calm voice as I could muster, to please release the door and let me out. While I listened to her vehement replies of "No! Only if I don't have to go with her!" I wondered what those dire consequences might be that Mrs. Hill was talking about. I then turned in the long narrow closet and walked down to the end.

The closet ran parallel to the hallway and one side of his classroom wall with another door at the other end, which opened onto the hall. Tanja, and most of the other children did not know this. I simply exited the closet this way and returned to the classroom via the main hallway. Before I walked back into the room, I took a few deep breaths. With the learning materials still in hand, I crossed the threshold into the classroom, and without missing a beat picked up my dialogue where I had left off, continuing to regale Mrs. Hill and Tanja with what they were to do in the learning assistance room.

Houdini could not have done better. Mrs. Hill attempted to regain her composure, but Tanja who was still braced against the closet door, was overwhelmed by my miraculous reappearance from the closet. She looked first at the door she held fast and then at me. Tanja's expression was one of complete perplexity. With her mouth opening and closing several times like that of a fish out of water she uttered, "How, how?" She could not bear it. She collapsed to the floor, with a loud scream and then came slow, almost pitiful, sobs. When she had finally exhausted her tears she went willingly with Mrs. Hill. It transpired that they had a wonderful time together. It wasn't the full time, but it was still a time that had some positive affect upon Tanja, as she was in good spirits when she returned and for the remainder of the day. She even apologized to me for attacking me and locking me in the closet.

Difference Is—Well, Different

Tanja was "different." In the language of the educational system, she was "special." Special education has its own language and conceptual framework. Its paramount objective is the integration of "special needs students" into the "regular classroom." School-based teams, which can be composed of principals, classroom teachers, counselors, parents or guardians, social services personnel, student support aids, speech pathologists, psychologists, and special education teachers, meet regularly to manage the progress of special needs students. Each individual educational plan (IEP) is written up collaboratively. Goals are set and eventually progress is assessed. If goals are not met, a new IEP is written.

Tanja was "special." What makes someone different? Or as in Tanja's circumstance as well as those of many other children, what made her special? Some people suggest it is the "other's" perception, but there seems to be something else. Tanja had no hold over her behavior nor many of her other emotional problems. Her IEP, its development and implementation set her apart and marked her difference. She was managed through medication, behavior programs, and education plans; she became a case to be managed; her humanity became secondary, perhaps even tertiary.

41

What can Tanja hope for? Was she not simply trying to gain some bit, some scrap, of control over her situation, herself, her story? And I, in our confrontation, with the power of being the teacher and the support of the school, would not acquiesce at that moment. In order, "to be nobody but yourself—in a world which is doing its best, night and day, to make you everybody else—means to fight the hardest battle which any human being can fight"(cummings, 1985, p. 97). All of us around Tanja focused on her behavior, syndrome, illness, while she grasped for her scraps of fragmented self.

My experience with children has lead me to think that the very young seldom hang on to non-abusive emotionally charged moments for very long after they occur. Tanja truly was very happy after going with Mrs. Hill that day. I, on the other hand, sit here now all these years later with this story. I don't know if I did the right thing that day. After telling this story, I'm thinking I probably should have done something different that day. I do know that I needed to other things in class with Tanja so that she could just be there while I tried to help her hold the space and tell her story. Tanja and I did that for the rest of the school year then she moved, again.

Getting Through the Year: Another Life Changing Story

A woman is looking through the window in the door trying to catch the teacher's attention. She is dressed in loose fitting blue jeans and a black cotton sweatshirt that is rather large for her slight frame. Mrs. Allie is her name and she is one of six parents who had volunteered to do this month's head check for lice on all the school's students and staff. She waits a few more minutes in the hopes that I would notice her through the window.

I was in the middle of telling a story and describing how the young heroine had thwarted the villainous attack by a neighboring country. My arms waved about my head as I painted the image of the bad guys forced to march home, defeated without having even engaged in battle. All their ships had been skewered on tall pikes driven into the harbor seabed. Then I proceeded to gambol about the classroom in an effort to depict their departure. Mrs. Allie waited until she was certain that he had finished the story. This was easy to do. She simply waited for my arms to stop waving about and for the children in the class to begin asking questions. A child began to ask, in a rather incredulous voice, "How could they have gotten everyone of the army ships stuck on a pointed pole?"

Mrs. Allie knocked and then opened the door. All the heads in the classroom turned toward her in a choreographic synchrony that would have been the envy of any dance troupe. "Excuse me, Mr. Lewis, I've come to let you know that we are ready to check the students in your class."

"Okay," I said. "How many can you take at a time?"

"Six."

I rattled off the names of six children, who sprang from their seats and scurried out the door behind Mrs. Allie. While the first six children were out of the room the remaining children quickly forgot about the story they had just been enthralled with and began to talk about lice. Some children were fascinated with the idea of bugs living on a person's head, as long as it wasn't their head. However, most of the children were apprehensive about having their heads checked. They seemed to know that there was a certain stigma associated with head lice. I quickly set to work to try to assuage the children's apprehension and dispel the notion that having head lice was bad or dirty.

I began by saying, "head lice are just little creatures that happen to enjoy living on the heads of human beings. Having head lice does not mean you're dirty or that you don't keep yourself clean enough." I even added: "Head lice like really clean hair, not dirty hair." Although I wasn't sure if that was accurate, it would help the task at hand. I proceeded to regale the children with the knowledge that anyone could have head lice. Little Matt said, "Yeah! My Dad's friend got them and they weren't just in his hair. He had them in his armpits, too!" A chorus of "Uuuuw yuck!" with a smattering of "That's gross!" erupted from the group of 7 and 8 year olds. Some loud giggles followed.

"There was a girl at my old school who had lice all the time! She had really dirty, gross hair," added Eddie.

"That's enough, please," I said in a feeble attempt to stem the rising tide of lousy revelations. "Lot's of people can get head lice. I have good friends who have had lice."

"Have you ever had head lice, Mr. Lewis?" asked Dawn.

I hesitated for a moment and then lied straight into the face of her question. "Yes, I have, Dawn," I said, casually thinking, "what can this hurt. It should help any of them who might have them."

The first six children returned with clean heads and the next six who were named trotted out the door to have their heads examined by six mothers who would have preferred to be just about anywhere else but there. The class talked a little more about lice, but eventually moved on to other activities. When the six children returned, one of them was in tears. It was Dawn. She had lice. Two of her friends, Ivy and Nancy, also had lice but did not seem as devastated by the news. They were trying to comfort Dawn with the knowledge that she was not alone. I endeavored to play down the impact of the school policy requiring that they go home and treat their hair and remove all nits before returning to school. This was the "Nit Free Policy."

Six more children left the room to have their heads checked. They returned with clean heads. I set the children to several tasks, not the least of which was the day's math review sheet. I then joined the last six children to have my own head checked for lice. When I returned to the classroom, I did so rather sheepishly. I stood by the chalkboard and asked for everyone's attention. "It would seem," I began haltingly, "that I, too, have head lice and will have to go home and have my hair treated." Everyone stopped fidgeting and making noise at this announcement. Even Dawn halted her sobs and seemed to cheer up. It didn't take long for the news of my infestation to spread to all the children in the school. It was accompanied by the knowledge that this was the *second* time I had them. To the incredulous "how do *you* know?" came the confident reply, "because *he* told us!"

This Is Lousy

I had told them I had had lice before in the hopes of removing or at least eclipsing the stigma they associated with lice. Stigma is a strange thing—wholly human in its origins and ubiquitous in nature. Stigma is a mark, a sign of disgrace or disease (Barber, 1998). I sense my own discomfort of being stigmatized. There are odd things in our behavior around "catching something," and those who have not caught it that transcends the realm of health and hygiene.

Now Dawn is in tears because she has already learned that she is seen differently with the arrival of head lice. However, Nancy and Ivy seem nonplussed. In fact they are more concerned with assuaging their friend's distress. I have lice. The news seems to shift things. Dawn's countenance is transformed and there is a barely appreciable shift in scope but it seems to change little about the dichotomy of perception: You have lice. You don't have lice. He is very ill. He is the picture of health. She lives in an old broken down bus. She lives in a mansion. Where is the parent involvement in his schooling? Both parents are very involved in his schooling. She always has a wholesome lunch. She rarely brings a lunch to school.

We look and *how* we see affects what we see. How do I perceive the children in my care? How did I perceive Tanja, Dawn and the several hundred other children who have interacted with me in the classroom over the past 20 years? What affect does that perception have upon them? How have my perception and their perception been shaped and formed? The Pygmalion effect is well known, but this is something else, not deeper, not peripheral, not transcendent. The tendency related to what is seen to inform reality is pervasive. It is the *sine qua non* of simplistic perception.

As easily as a louse attaching itself to a hair, our place in the world is determined by our own and others' perception. To be a good teacher, I need to be attentive to how I perceive the children in my care; how I perceive myself and how they perceive me, but most importantly, how they perceive themselves. Perception becomes fundamental to our construction and formation of meaning and understanding, yet so often perception itself prevents us from seeing some important aspect about existence, both our own and others. Perception is a cousin to routine and ritual, which tend to provide set meanings so that the unknown, uncertainty or ambiguity does not overwhelm us. However, that so often limits our view, sometimes promoting myopic ways of being and knowing. "The world as revealed to us through the structure of perception and knowledge is the product of our activity, and our words are at once the mementos of our past actions and the premise of our future ones" (Grumet, 1978, p. 40). Rituals and routines appear to prescribe what to do so that we do not have to wonder. Through our everyday routines and rituals, we evade instances of doubt and moments of not knowing what to do. Something of consequence is embedded in our routines, rituals and communicative interactions, which are so pushed toward the background that we don't see it. Operating without that awareness I am not cognizant of the creative force inherent in my own and others' words, actions, and routines in the classroom. Perhaps a good teacher needs to act and speak with an awareness that acknowledges this creative force latent in words and actions so that he or she might find what it is that resides outside routines, rituals, words and perception and be present with the children in their care.

REFERENCES

Barber, K. (Ed.). (1998). *Oxford English Dictionary.* Toronto: Oxford University Press.

Cummings, E. E. (1985). Letter to a high school editor, 1955. In G. Seldes (Ed.), *The great thoughts* (p. 97). New York: Ballantine Books.

Grumet, M. (1978). Curriculum as theater: Merely players. *Curriculum Inquiry, 8,* 38–64.

Grumet, M. (1991). Curriculum and the art of daily life. In G. Willis & W. H. Schubert (Eds.), *Reflections form the heart of education inquiry* (pp. 74–89). New York: SUNY.

JEFF DAITSMAN

6. THE TEACHER WITH THE BEARD

A Nurturing Male Helps Children Overcome Bias

I walked into a preschool classroom for the first time since I had decided to become a teacher. I was there to do an observation for one of my first Child Development classes at Truman College. I had few memories of my own experience in preschool from when I was a child, and I was excited to see what the class would be like. I vividly recall the room, with several tables where lunch was being set up near the entrance. The room was L-shaped, with the bend being at the far end from the entrance. Around the corner were several children playing with connecting blocks at a table. All throughout the room there were shelves filled with toys. In the main part of the room, right next to the bend, there was a bookshelf and a large rug with a CD player on the floor next to it.

The teacher gathered the children on the rug and started the CD. For the first time, I heard what I would later find would be a universal child favorite, "We're Going on a Bear Hunt." I stomped and swished and climbed with the children, and enjoyed myself a great deal. I laughed with the children and we overall enjoyed ourselves. I felt right at home in this classroom, and I knew that I had made the right choice in deciding to become a teacher.

As the children went to go eat lunch, the teachers invited me to join them. I recall particularly enjoying the corn. As I finished up my lunch and prepared to leave, the teacher came over to me and told me something I'll never forget. "The kids seemed to really enjoy having you here. I think it's great that you want to be a teacher," her expression changed ever so slightly as she said what was ultimately on her mind, "but you might want to consider shaving your beard before applying for any teaching jobs." Her speech became faster as she continued to explain to me how directors and parents might view me, but I was so thrown off by her comment that I was only half listening by this point.

Shave my beard, I thought, but it's so much a part of who I am. Why would I want to shave my beard? Why does it matter how these adults view me when it's the children who will be interacting with me the most? As I left the school, I continued to reflect on her statement. I recalled my own childhood and my favorite adult outside of my family. Rick had a long black beard and long curly hair. He would always play games with my sister and me; take the time to explain his video games to us; allowed us to push the limits beyond what our parents permit. My memories of him are those of being both fun and caring. My most vivid memory of Rick is of one

W.Watson and C.S.Woods (eds), Go Where You Belong:
Cultural Workers in the Lives of Children, Families, and Communities, 47–53.

Halloween when he set up a system in which there was an electric light within the pumpkin on the front porch which was hooked into a speaker system with a microphone in our second floor apartment. Whenever somebody would speak into the microphone the pumpkin would light up. I was in awe of this man who would go to such lengths for a holiday that is primarily designed for children.

Now that I was an adult, recalling these experiences in my childhood with this man who was so important to me, it occurred to me for the first time that my hair and beard, while not the same color as Rick's, had taken on the same style. Had this been a subconscious tribute to the man I had loved as a child? Or did it reflect a similarity in personality style that I would choose the same hairstyle as Rick? Regardless of why my facial hairstyle, it was clear to me that it would not detract from my relationships with the children.

It was also clear to me that there exists in society a bias against men working with children. The implication of the teacher's statement about my beard is that some adults believe that having facial hair can detract from building relationships with children. Yet when children interact with pets there is a calming effect when they stroke the fur. Softness is soothing to young children. Males tend to have a good deal more body hair than women, adding a layer of softness beyond the skin. So why, then, is there a bias against the natural physical softness of men?

Reasons for Anti-male Bias in Preschool

Perhaps this bias stems from existing social stereotypes of the roles of men and women. Kindlon and Thompson (2000) speak of "a steady diet of commercials in which a man is not a man unless he is tough, drives a tough truck, and drinks lots of beer" (p. 15). Men are supposed to be tough, and softness is not something that seems to fit into that framework. As a result, when people speak of male physicality, they tend to overlook the softness that is naturally present.

Women, on the other hand, are viewed in the role of the nurturing mother, so much so that one of my female co-workers when I was a swimming teacher once told me she believed that behaviors exhibited by children in her infant/toddler swimming class were different than ones she assumed were exhibited in my infant/toddler classes because "women are naturally nurturing" (when I asked her to clarify the different behaviors, she described the same sorts of behaviors I observed in my own swimming classes). What she meant by nurturing, in this context, was the female ability to breast-feed. This perception that a person cannot be nurturing without being in possession of female body parts could also lead to the mental blindness to the softness of the male body.

Or perhaps this blindness can be attributed to fear. Ashcraft & Sevier (2006) discuss the idea put forth by Sarah Farquhar that "being labeled... a 'child molester'... is a not uncommon experience or concern for many male elementary teachers" (p. 131). I myself have encountered this fear. Every place I have worked with children, I have been cautioned to greater or lesser degrees about physical contact with the children (i.e. hands visible at all times, no hugs, no sitting in laps, etc.), cautions that I've been told by some female teachers they have never heard. There have been times as I am sitting with a female child and she begins absent-mindedly stroking my arm hair when my mind turns to these warnings. If someone were to see a girl caressing a man in this manner there would be a tendency to assume something of a sexual nature.

Indeed, these fears are not unfounded. Marotz, Cross, & Rush (2005) point out that, "More often, the perpetrator [of sexual abuse] is male and not a stranger to the child, but rather someone the child knows and trusts, for example a… teacher" (p. 280). However, this tendency for the perpetrators of sexual abuse to be males stems from a failure to develop a healthy attitude toward emotional relationships. Kindlon & Thompson (2000) reveal that "[t]he majority of boys are not prepared to manage the complexities of a loving relationship because they've been short-changed on the basic skills of emotional literacy" (p. 197). Boys are taught to detach from emotional connection, being socialized to believe that these are characteristics only possessed by girls. Exhibiting these characteristics can result in insults from their peers. Serriere (2009) describes how, even in diverse settings, "there was generally a main group of boys who subtly enforced the norms of being a 'real boy'" (p. 21). This socialization stems from the existence of male dominance in society, and as Boldt (1996) puts it, "to be a boy associated with girls' interests and desires is construed as a step away from power and possibility" (p. 119).

This is why it is so important for young children to see men in nontraditional roles such as teachers. In order for boys to grow up to have healthy attitudes toward emotions and relationships, they must understand that men can be nurturing. As young children, they need to interact with males who exhibit such qualities in order to see it as an ideal to be emulated. Without nurturing male role models, the image of the male popularized by the media of strength, aggression, and emotional vacuum is the one that boys will come to emulate.

The Seasonal Beard

If I were to take that teacher's advice and shave off my beard, I would have not only missed out on showing a softer side to men, but I also would have missed out on many opportunities for children to become more consciously aware of the similarities between men and women. My beard is seasonal. This means that I shave it off on the first day of spring and remain clean-shaven throughout spring and summer. However, on the first day of fall, I stop shaving so that by the time temperatures drop as winter approaches, I have grown enough facial hair to provide insulation against the Chicago winter. The children learn a little bit about the seasons from this, but more notably the children learn about gender roles.

For children who see men every day without beards, views of the differences between men and women rarely surface to the level of conscious thought. When the children meet me at the beginning of the school year, and I am clean shaven with long hair, there is no discussion of the similarity of my appearance to the stereotypical image of a woman. However, as they watch my beard grow the children slowly become accustomed to a new image of me that includes a beard so that when I shave it off in March, it sparks a great deal of discussion. Having grown accustomed to the beard and seeing it shaved off makes children much more conscious of my

49

appearance, and they begin to note the similarity between my new look and that of women that they know.

The comment, "You look like a girl" made by children, becomes commonplace for several weeks and elicits a good deal of discussion where the children are able to take a closer look at their own biases and form a new framework of understanding the roles of men and women. This discussion returns on a deeper level when summer approaches and I begin putting my hair in a ponytail.

I recall one 3-year-old boy whose initial reaction to seeing me with a ponytail was to tell me that only girls wear ponytails. I explained to him that anybody with long hair can wear a ponytail and that I tied my hair back so that my neck didn't get too hot. The next day he came in telling me that he had put his hair in a ponytail at home. Because of his hair length, I was inwardly skeptical that this had actually occurred, but I nonetheless discussed it with him as if it had, encouraging his desire to look beyond his previous stereotyped view of gender. When his father came in to pick him up, I told him of this discussion, and he confirmed that he had put his son's hair in a ponytail at the son's request. The following day the child came in with a little ponytail sprouting out from the top of his head.

How I Became a Teacher

When asked why I chose to become a teacher, I usually respond by telling the story of how I found myself babysitting for the director of the theatre company I worked for. This led me to deciding that I wanted to work with children as a career. However, nothing in life is so simplistic that it can be boiled down that easily or at least for me to state it that easily. It takes a nurturing disposition to be a preschool teacher. My position requires of me to be attuned to changes in development and be ready to guide children as they learn. At times, I act as a substitute for the parent, and I am prepared to accommodate the child when he or she is feeling lonely or upset and seeking comfort. I simply must be someone that the children can respect and trust. It is only when children feel that they are in a safe environment that they are able to realize their full potential, and as an early childhood educator, it is my job to create such an environment. To do so, I must have a nurturing character.

The values I learned growing up gave me such a character. I grew up surrounded by strong women and nurturing men. In my early years of school, I found myself puzzled by the behaviors of aggressive boys. The summer camp that I went to as a child was often referred to lovingly as a "hippie camp" and was the purveyor of a variety of gender roles that are outside of the norm. My mannerisms and outlook sometimes led my peers to believing I was also gay despite my heterosexual preferences. My atypical views of gender normativity made me an outsider in many social groupings in junior high and high school. I found my social niche with activists and thespians. I chose to make theater my career, and about a year after I graduated high school, I found myself designing lights for a theatre company that wrote musicals and put on performances in deliberate defiance of mainstream gender stereotypes. I became the company's resident technical director and lighting designer.

Since I was a "techie," and not always directly involved in the rehearsal process, I would often end up babysitting for the director during rehearsals. I found nurturing and caring for children was something that I was good at and also found very rewarding. I became as another member of the family. When the company disbanded many years after I joined them, I decided that I would go back to school and major in Early Childhood Education. However, I encountered bias at the first university I attended. I recall the first education class I took. The instructor, impressed by my grasp of the subject matter, told me after several weeks of meeting that I no longer needed to attend class. I continued attending nonetheless and tutoring my (all female) classmates, most of whom were elementary education majors. Well into the semester, the teacher told me that, because I was a man, I should think about working with older children than preschool.

I chose to transfer to a different college. The summer after I took that class, I began my first real job working with children. I worked as a counselor back at my old summer camp. The children were all elementary school age, but I was placed in the youngest unit. Yet even at this progressive camp, I found that some children had similar biases to those that had baffled me as a child.

"Are You Gay?"

I recall one particular series of interactions with a child from outside of my unit at this camp. He had been coming to the camp for several years already and had been impacted by the camp's social justice curriculum. He understood, in theory, that gender had many expressions and that people shouldn't be judged by how they choose to express their gender and sexual preferences. As with most of the children at the camp, he enjoyed spending time with many counselors, including myself.

I recall sitting on the deck outside the farmhouse before or after meals with a deck of cards, teamed up against another camper and counselor in an intense game of Euchre as other children gathered around to watch and cheer on one team or another, or even just to observe and learn how the game was played. I recall other times that I would be in that crowd of observers, staring and listening in awe when this particular child would show off his impressive drumming skills.

During mealtimes, he would often choose to sit at my table. I recall one day at lunchtime a child asked a question about a gay staff member. Though I can no longer remember what it was that I specifically said in response to the question, I do recall that it could have been misinterpreted to mean that I myself was gay as well. The child who enjoyed spending so much time with me suddenly seemed taken aback. He inched away from the head of the table where I was sitting and looked askance at me.

He confronted me with the question, wanting to clarify whether or not I was indeed gay. As he asked this, I could tell he was uncomfortable with the idea that this adult male that he looked up to and spent so much time with could be attracted to men. I decided that the best way to help him to internalize his theoretical open-mindedness was to leave the question of my sexual preference unanswered until he learned to accept me regardless of my answer. He continued to spend time with me, but he wouldn't sit as close as he used to, and his facial expressions were different when I was around.

This continued for several days, but soon he began to relax around me once more. He learned to accept me for who I was and his demeanor returned to normal. He continued to enjoy spending time with me, playing cards or showing off his drumming skills. When I finally "came out of the closet" as a heterosexual he was surprised, but there was no change to our relationship this time. He had truly internalized his non-judgmental attitude and was no longer phased by something that he had long been saying doesn't make a difference to our friendship.

Moving Beyond Bias

We live in a society full of biases, and in order to overcome them, we need to give children the opportunity to examine what biases they have developed. Pelo and Davidson (2000) list four often-published goals of an anti-bias curriculum:
- Nurture each child's construction of a knowledgeable, confident self-identity and group identity.
- Promote each child's comfortable, empathetic interaction with people from diverse backgrounds.
- Foster each child's critical thinking about bias.
- Cultivate children's ability to stand up for themselves and for others in the face of bias (pp. 4–6).

I feel that much of these goals can be accomplished very simply by exposing children to diverse populations, including diversity of gender. The more children are forced to confront their own assumptions and stereotyped perceptions, the more they will be able to move past them.

I recently studied a year and a half of my students' story dictations looking at how they develop and express their understanding of gender. I found gender to be a social construct, but more importantly I found that attempts to ignore the existence of and avoid discussion of gender stereotypes served only to reinforce and strengthen their proliferation. Gonzalez-Mena stresses a major part of dealing with issues of diversity as being self-reflection. "Self-reflection can reveal deep pain, insecurities, fears, and all manner of hidden feelings" (p. 54). As a male teacher, I am able to get children to reflect on their gender biases in ways that would be difficult or next to impossible if they only had female teachers in the classroom.

As a society, we need to encourage men to take on more nurturing roles overall. We need to expose children to men who are not constrained by the stereotypes that society provides. It is my hope that the children in my care will grow up with dis-positions that can open up possibilities for a better future. Perhaps someday my male students will be making a choice similar to mine, deciding whether to take on a career in a nurturing field or whether to go into something deemed more appropriate for "men." They likely will not remember me when this happens, but I anticipate that their experiences today of questioning stereotypes and bias will help them to make this choice with an open mind.

REFERENCES

Ashcraft, C., & Sevier, B. (2006). Gender will find a way: exploring how male elementary teachers make sense of their experiences and responsibilities. *Contemporary Issues in Early Childhood, 7*(2), 130–145.

Boldt, G. M. (1996). Sexist and heterosexist responses to gender bending in an elementary classroom. *Curriculum Inquiry, 26*(2), 113–131.

Gonzalez-Mena, J. (2005). *Diversity in early care and education: Honoring differences* (4th ed.). New York: McGraw-Hill.

Kindlon, D., & Thompson, M. (2000). *Raising Cain: Protecting the emotional life of boys.* New York: Random House.

Marotz, L. R., Cross, M. Z., & Rush, J. M. (2005). *Health, safety, and nutrition for the young child* (6th ed.). Clifton Park, NY: Thomson Delmar Learning.

Pelo, A., & Davidson, F. (2000). *That's not fair! A teacher's guide to activism with young children.* St. Paul, MN: Redleaf Press.

Serriere, S. C. (2009). The making of "masculinity": The impact of symbolic and physical violence on students, Pre-K and beyond. *Democracy and Education, 18*(1). 21–27.

DANIEL CASTNER

7. IT'S A MAN'S FIELD TOO

Men as Care Givers

I recall my first year teaching kindergarten and being approached by a parent on the first day of school who joked that she was expecting the teacher to be a "sweet little old lady wearing a denim jumper who enjoys knitting sweaters for her grandchildren," and was surprised to get to school and find a "big, young guy who barely looks a day over twenty and would blend right in at a frat party." I laughed at the witty remark and have repeatedly acknowledged that I surely look nothing like most of the children's preschool teachers. Now, ten years later, when parents and teaching colleagues find out that I am pursuing doctoral studies, they make the common assumption that I must be striving to become an administrator. I have frequently heard remarks such as: "since you've been teaching for a while you must be ready to take over and be the boss" that I have learned to explain upfront my commitment to practicing, studying and researching early childhood education.

The abundance of conversations similar to those described above has provided a near constant reminder of the scarcity of men in early childhood classrooms. This scarcity of men has lead to common images of early childhood educators and common assumptions about the few men whose vocation is to teach young children. I will indeed never look like a sweet old lady that so many people imagine will be caring for the children. However, as my hair begins to gray and my face acquires new wrinkles, I am beginning to look more like the authority figure that so many people assume will be managing sweet old ladies.

These familiar images and regular assumptions create socially constructed hurdles of gender bias that men need to overcome in order to be accepted as competent and caring early childhood educators. In his book *Uncommon Caring*, King (1998) expresses his concern that "when primary education is viewed in a context of caring, men's work as caregivers can be seen as a problem" (p. 3–4). King (1998) draws upon the work of Noddings and Gilligan as key referents to primary education being viewed in a context of caring. King's (1998) work serves as an illustrative representation of the challenges that many men face in what he calls "a complex culture that is female, even feminine, but decidedly non-feminist" (p. 12).

Through my personal experiences as a man who teaches kindergarten, I will acknowledge and confirm King's (1998) assertions that onlookers often perceive of men's care giving efforts as being suspect. Since I am not a female, nor I am

W.Watson and C.S.Woods (eds), Go Where You Belong:
Cultural Workers in the Lives of Children, Families, and Communities, 55–62.

feminine, many have been suspicious enough of my choice to work as a caregiver that they have assumed that I will soon take on the more masculine role of an administrator. Additionally, I will expand upon King's (1998) later claim by describing my challenges as a man struggling to advocate for changes in "a complex culture that is female, even feminine, but decidedly non-feminist" (p. 12).

My experiences as a kindergarten teacher, in certain ways, confirm King's assumption that onlookers often perceive men's care giving efforts as being suspect. While I have also experienced being excluded from the customary image of an "ordinary kindergarten teacher," the most common assumptions are not that I am an inadequate caregiver, but rather that I am in the process of becoming "the boss." In this way, I do not struggle to be accepted as a male caregiver. Instead, I face the challenge of all early childhood educators of having my caring activities diminished as being an inferior form of professional competency among the various roles of educators at my elementary school. The intellectual acumen and the professional skills of early childhood educators are often disregarded as semi-professional activities because they cannot be generalized to traditionally "male-defined" ways of knowing.

Both Gilligan (1982) and Noddings (1984) advance a relational ethic as a feminine attribute with a long history of being devalued in a male-defined patriarchal society. Noddings' (1984) *Caring* and Gilligan's (1982) *In a different voice* push forward the underrepresented experiences of women. These feminist scholars do not lay claim to acts of receptivity, relatedness, and responsiveness as labor solely carried out by women. But, they suggest that these ways of being are of worthy intellectual and moral merit. Noddings' (1984) feminine ethic of care and Gilligan's (1982) insights into the way that women consider a web of relationship as the basis for moral decision illuminate long-established female traditions often exemplified intuitively by compassionate early childhood educators. While these two scholars have raised feminine perspectives to important new consideration through a theoretical lens, our practical educational system lags behind in achieving gender balance.

Levine, Murphy and Wilson (1994) note that a "dimension of diversity is valuing the interests and talents of both sexes, of recognizing the contributions that both women and men can make to children, and to one another in their work with children" (p. 10). As mentioned above, *a feminine ethic* of care is a traditionally female contribution to the lives of children in our schools. The feminine perspective of a relationship-oriented moral reasoning has a 25 year theoretical history of serving as the basis for understanding a pedagogy of care. Yet, the work of caring too often goes unexamined, unnoticed or misunderstood in the best early childhood classrooms.

Feeling at odds with the dominant practices of classroom management and school discipline have lead me to an interest in studying the complexities of nurturing the social, emotional and moral development of young children. I have become dedicated to reflective inquiries that refine these affective attributes of my pedagogy. Questioning customary ideas about disciplining children has helped me establish a critical distance from the conventional behaviorist techniques of enforcing a fixed set of classroom or school rules through the use of punishments and rewards. As an alternative, I work diligently to have a classroom atmosphere that embodies democratic principles. I share power, control and responsibilities with the children by facilitating frequent and regular classroom meetings. During these meetings the children discusses matters of interest, importance, or concern to them. The children voice concerns, share insights, offer each other advice and support. The focus is not on obedience to my directives; but rather we concentrate on sharing the responsibilities that enable possibilities in our classroom for fairness and flourishing.

Despite my ongoing inquiries and interests in democratic and caring classroom communities, many of my colleagues assume that children in my class have success because of an adherence to traditional classroom practices. For example, a few years ago, a little boy in my class with Asperger syndrome was having a difficult time transitioning into kindergarten. In late September, he garnered the attention of many of my colleagues as he got off the bus. Jared would yell, "I don't want to come to school! I hate this place! I don't want to get into trouble! I want to go home!"

An administrative colleague noticed the commotion and approached me to offer customary advice to address the situation. Her perspective was aligned with the dominant male-defined Kohlbergian conception of a young child's development. She perceived Jared, and any other kindergarten-aged child for that matter, as dependent of external rules and authority. From that viewpoint, she believed that the best way to support Jared's success was to give clear directions and to concisely state what the consequence will be for disobedience. With Noddings (1984) "feminine ethic of care" as a basis for how I understood the child's needs and my role as a caring educator teacher, the situation played out in the following way as I recorded them on a daily notepad.

September 27, 2006

Jared came to school today in a sour mood. He said that he didn't like school and wanted to stay home. Furthermore, he hated problems and didn't want to be here for all the problems.

We had a meeting so Jared could explain his feelings and see if his classmates had any helpful ideas. It turned out that Jared was horrified by our regular practice of coming to the carpet to discuss classroom problems. He assumed that if he had a problem that the discussion would lead to him "being in trouble." I clarified to Jared that the point of the discussion was not to punish someone with a problem, but to help that person. I then explained that he had the problem of not being happy at school. Now that we knew this, maybe we could help.

The children began with suggestions such as, "I'll play dinosaurs with you during recess. Jared liked the idea but said that it still did not solve his problem. He said that he liked presents and maybe we could give him a dinosaur as a present.

Steven. said, "Well I could draw one for you. I think he and I were both a little surprised at how well Jared received the suggestion. Both Steven and Jared looked to me for approval and I was already getting paper and crayons out from the writing center. Many of the other children asked if they could also make a green dinosaur for Jared. Jared went home with a pile of dinosaur pictures and a feeling that he is an important member of our class.

September 28, 2006

Jared came in this morning with animal stickers for everyone. He said, "Thanks everyone for making me pictures. I brought animal stickers and I want everyone to have one."

It seemed to be his way to say thank you. I received two emails from his parents thanking me for taking the extra time to console Jared. They mentioned that the pictures made a world of difference. Jared went home and told his mom and dad about all of his friends at school and how they helped him.

Although Jared's parents thanked me, all that I did was to allow his classmates the time and opportunity to care. The children's expression of care was more powerful and meaningful to Jared than anything that I could have ever done or said. He needed to know that our classroom is a place where he is important and that his feelings matter. He needed to know that we care. His classmates expressed their care to him yesterday, through their actions. Today, Jared reciprocated.

My colleague noticed that the problem did not persist and asked how I "extinguished the behavior." Expecting a description of how I laid down the law with the threat of consequences for noncompliance that Jared would dread, my colleague was surprised to hear the above story. My colleague suspected that the succinct resolution must be the result of a much-needed presence of my masculine authority. Further, she recommended that we could devise a behavior plan if "further problems" arose.

However, I quickly rebutted that I believed that she was missing the mark in thinking that Jared needed to be dissuaded from creating problems. He was already so petrified of having a problem that he couldn't think of anything to do by crying and yelling. He needed to be assured that when problems arise, his classroom was a safe place that would support and appreciate his best efforts. He didn't need the strong arm of authority to keep him in bounds. He needed to build a support system of trusting, caring relationships, so he would not be afraid to try. Therefore, I was upfront in telling this administrative colleague that I was uninterested in implementing a strategy with a behaviorist-orientation. I was assertive in defending my intentions of using the alternative approach described above should other problems arise.

What is ironic in this case is that my female, administrative colleague and I contradict our theoretical gender-defined tendencies. I took on the female-defined orientation of focusing on relationships, while she adopted the male-defined perspective of concentrating on upholding rules. My frustration was not that I was excluded to a female-defined role; rather, I was confronted with the, unfamiliar to me, struggle of trying to advancing a traditionally feminine way of knowing in a male-defined hegemony. Perplexed, I began observing, my female teaching colleagues whom I considered to be compassionate care givers. The following narratives describe the ways that they each faced the challenges of a gender-biased educational system.

A Year Later, Stacy Smiles and Nods

As part of Jared's Individualized Education Program (IEP) he has a behavior plan that focuses on positive reinforcement. For each cooperative action and for each completion of an academic task, Jared's teacher is to give him a ticket. After a certain amount of tickets had been accumulated, Stacy, his teacher, would give him a reward or special treat. Trusting that this course of action was carefully planned to meet Jared's needs, Stacy began to implement the plan.

Immediately Stacy became concerned about how Jared paid more attention to the tickets than the task at hand. He was a nervous wreck that he would make a mistake and not earn a ticket. Soon, Stacy saw no other choice but to abandon the plan. She pulled Jared aside and told him that she was concerned about how nervous the tickets were making him. She had decided to forget about the tickets. Jared thanked her as he watched her throw the tickets into the trashcan. After this, a strong teacher-student relationship began to form and Jared made great progress in the classroom.

Stacy tried to explain her decision to other members of the IEP team. She was reminded that an IEP is a legal document that needed to be followed to the letter. Furthermore, it was suggested that Jared would eventually become accustomed to the ticket system if Stacy remained committed and stuck to it. Unwilling to torture a student with this socio-emotional game, Stacy remained committed to her caring ways of supporting Jared in the classroom.

A few months later, at a formal IEP meeting, Stacy was asked how the behavior plan was working. "Just fine. He has made great social growth this year. Thanks for all of your help." Other similar examples follow which demonstrates the lack of care when dealing with children with regards to gender.

Mary Goes Undercover

At first, Mary thought that Cliff's temper tantrums were more than she could handle in her first grade classroom. She knew about some recent challenges and changes that had occurred in his home life. She empathized with what she realized was a six-year-old boy in emotional distress. Still, she worried about the other children. What would they go home and say about this boy who yelled and once even kicked their teacher. Also, she knew that she had to protect Cliff's classmates from his often-unpredictable, sometimes physical, tirades.

Traditional interventions were suggested that included behavior charts and reward systems. Mary was told to document all incidents. She was informed that 15 weeks of behavioral incidents needed to be documented as a requisite to placing him in a classroom for children with emotional disturbances. The behavior chart that was portrayed to Cliff as an incentive program was also a weapon that would record his every misstep as part of the process of getting rid of him. This was all handed to Mary with the pessimistic warning to be prepared for a long and challenging 15 weeks.

Soon Mary saw the behavior chart as little more than a distraction. She began building a relationship with Cliff and appreciated how hard he would try to control his temper. The more their relationship grew the more superficial their conversations at the behavior chart seemed to feel. Mary discarded the behavior chart. She also decided that although Cliff was not without incident at school, she would not document minor offenses. She did this first because she did not want a collection of minor incidents to be used against Cliff. Secondly, Mary knew that the response to her referral forms would be directives to implement a variation of the behavior chart. She said, "sometimes it is best to fly under the radar, instead of getting ordered to do something that you know won't work."

Sally's Compromise

After Jerry was sent home for fleeing the building, Sally, another teacher, received the standard directions for a behavior chart intervention. Upon receiving this advice she voiced her concern that this intervention did not address Jerry's specific needs. Further, she questioned the efficacy of the reward system that she has seen fail so many children in the past. In return for sharing her concerns and asking for other suggestions, Sally only received condescending encouragement. They told her, "I know that it is stressful to have a difficult student. Just hang in there and give it your best try." Sally lamented, "I know it isn't going to work but I have to do it because they suggested it. But, I'm going to have to find other things to do with him because the behavior chart isn't going to help."

On her own, Sally collected and reviewed literature on classroom guidance. Much of the constructivist oriented resources resonated with her existing beliefs about young children and the teaching and learning process. Sally remains perplexed by the ongoing juggling act of balancing her obedience to school authorities and her evolving professional understanding of constructivist teaching practices.

Noddings (2003) describes teaching as a relational practice. Embedded in this relational practice are the essential needs to nurture the emotional basis of learning (Denham, 2006) and to appreciate the necessity of facilitating supportive peer relationships (Ladd, Herald & Andrews, 2006). Enacting a relational practice also requires a teacher to make careful inferences regarding the "inner states" of the thinking, feeling and being that informs each child's moral development (Johansson, 2006). By recognizing the social, emotional and moral foundations of teaching, early childhood educators put into practice a particular professional knowledge base and skill set. Nonetheless, enhancing this knowledge base and skill set through professional development opportunities seems to present greater demands for my colleagues who are striving to take up an ethic of care in their classrooms. The challenges of making caring relations a top priority in early childhood classrooms is complicated for men and women by a historical marginalization of women's ways of knowing.

The moral virtue of nurturing children steers our shared belief that it is the professional responsibility of "the teacher to set an example with her whole self—her intellect, her responsiveness, her humor, her curiosity... her care" (Noddings, 2003, p. 244). To use their intellect, responsiveness, humor and curiosity my colleagues felt a need to intentionally maintain privacy in their classrooms. When administrators and psychologists espouse behaviorist practices, these teachers have learned that the path of least resistance is a deceptive, yet compliant nod. Therefore, these knowledgeable educators decide to disengage in public collegial discourse. Consequently, the important work of guiding teachers' most caring and responsive decisions is hidden behind closed classroom doors; the walls of their classroom confine their leadership.

As I notice many teachers deciding to disengage in public collegial conversations, I began thinking about why so many of my most knowledgeable and talented colleagues would take such a passive leadership stance. What will the future hold for children if inclusive and caring teaching practices are only used secretively at our school? Furthermore, what will the future of the teaching profession hold if many of the most thoughtful educational practitioners are excluded from professional discourses by their own facades of consensus? As I advocate for a feminine ethic of care as an alternative to strict authoritarian styles of discipline, hidden issues of gender bias are unveiled. Some of my colleagues suggest that it is surely easier for me to share power because the implicit authority of my masculine presence. Others, like Mary, understand and even applaud my commitment to caring pedagogical practices but advise that I should "fly under the radar" to avoid difficult ideological confrontations that disturb our traditional colleagues.

Goodwin and Genor (2008) remind us that "each person comes to teaching with preconceptions that need to be consciously examined and deliberately disturbed" (p. 202). In this light, perhaps more important than recruiting more men to early childhood classrooms, it is that men and women in the field have open discussions that challenge their historically-rooted and socially constructed beliefs about gender issues. If my school is to accomplish a gender-balanced educational experience, we can no longer have professionals' "flying under the radar." The feminine perspective is apparent when my colleagues seek to preserve the connectivity of their relationships with co-workers even at the cost of stifling their professional voice. However Lever (as cited in Gilligan, 1982) suggests that perhaps my unique masculine socialization has taught me to be more comfortable breaking away from others at work and contesting colleagues with competing points of view in challenging conversations. The question is not "have we as professionals disturbed each other's deeply held beliefs and understandings"; rather, "can we find ways to carefully disturbed one another enough?" Ultimately, Gilligan (1982) proposes that "These disparate visions in their tension reflect the paradoxical truths of human experience—that we know ourselves as separate only insofar as we live in connection with others, and that we experience relationship only insofar as we differentiate other from self" (p. 63). Such contributions can lead to more gender-balanced curriculum practices for our students and an avenue for all early childhood educators to be more fully human in their professional practices.

REFERENCES

Denham, S. (2006). The emotional basis of learning and development in early childhood education. In Spodek & Saracho (Ed.), *The handbook of research on the education of young children* (pp. 85–103). New Jersey: Lawrence Earlbaum Associates, Inc.

Gilligan, C. (1982). *In a different voice: Psychological theory and women's development.* Cambridge, MA: Harvard University Press.

Goodwin, A. L., & Genor, M. (2008). Disrupting the taken-for-granted: Autobiographical analysis in preservice teacher education. In Genishi & Goodwin (Ed.), *Diversity in early childhood education: Rethinking and doing* (pp. 201–218). New York: Routledge.

Johansson, E. (2006). Children's morality: Perspectives and research. In Spodek & Saracho (Ed.), *The handbook of research on the education of young children* (pp. 55–85). New Jersey: Lawrence Earlbaum Associates, Inc.

King, J. R. (1998). *Uncommon caring: Learning from men who teach young children.* New York: Teachers College Press.

Ladd, G. W., Herald, S. L., & Andrews, R. K. (2006). Young children's peer relations and social competence. In Spodek & Saracho (Ed.), *The handbook of research on the education of young children* (pp. 23–54). New Jersey: Lawrence Earlbaum Associates, Inc.

Levine, J. A., Murphy, D. T., & Wilson, S. (1993). *Getting men involved.* New York: Scholastic.

Noddings, N. (1984). *Caring: A feminine approach to ethics and moral education.* Berkeley, CA: University of California Press.

Noddings, N. (2003). Is teaching a practice? *Journal of Philosophy of Education, 37*(2), 241–251.

JUAN SANCHEZ

8. OPPORTUNITY FOR A DEPOSIT

Serving Children Linguistically

The skies were crystal clear and the light breeze was brisk. The weather was cool enough to wear a light jacket. That was a refreshingly welcome change compared to the heat and humidity typical of Chicago summers. I had arrived at my job before five a.m. as customary. It was an absolutely glorious early September morning and operations at Chicago's Midway airport were at full speed. However, unknown to us all, amid the bright sunshine and splendor of that Tuesday morning, a sinister plan had been set in motion; a plan that would alter the course of history and have lasting effects on the lives of many. By midday of September 11, 2001, I was standing in a microcosm of what was that fateful day. The place that I had been accustomed to be chock full of hustle and bustle, activity, people moving to and fro, arriving and leaving, business meetings, family reunions, vacations getaways was reduced to be desolate, eerily silent, and abandoned.

This was the genesis of my journey into the elementary education field. As a direct result of the events of September 11, 2001 the aviation industry suffered immense financial damage. Government bailouts, bankruptcy filings and liquidations were norms within the fiscally drained carriers' corporate portfolios. After four years of battling creditors and increased competition and radically declining revenues, my position was added to the ever growing causality list of job cuts, department eliminations, and downsizing.

I happened to see an article in a newspaper discussing the need for bilingual teachers. I immediately was intrigued by the notion of teaching. I had trained many of my staff and had some experience in the art of transferring knowledge to another person. I enjoyed the classroom setting and felt more than comfortable engaging adults in productive and constructive learning environments. In addition, I always felt that I had something to give back to the community. I especially felt drawn to the youth. Being a city resident, I saw the adversity that many of the young people had to face just to survive everyday life in their neighborhoods. I had experienced much of the same during my high school years. I knew that I could be a positive influence in their lives, a living role model. Someone they could identify with and possibly gain some inspiration from what I had accomplished in my life.

I also could relate to their experience as a bilingual student, as I too was enrolled in a bilingual program. This was my opportunity to set up a new path. As a result, I knew

W.Watson and C.S.Woods (eds), Go Where You Belong:
Cultural Workers in the Lives of Children, Families, and Communities, 63–66.
© 2011 Sense Publishers. All rights reserved.

that this would be a natural fit for me. I applied for an alternative certification program. This program allowed professionals with college degrees from sectors outside of education to transition to the classroom while pursuing certification through graduate level coursework in education. After reviewing my work history and past education, I was accepted into the program and began my classes.

Is There a Guy in the House?

I arrived at my school building and hurried quickly to the office. I had just been hired the previous day and that nervous feeling—much like a child who attends a new school for the first time—had yet to pass. I was eager to receive the keys to my room to set up my things, create a learning environment, set tables in cooperative groups, display print literature in abundance in all of the space, and all the other wonderful things I had learned in my three classes that I had taken up to this point. I had three days to prepare for the 27 students who would inhabit this space for the next 174 school days.

As I turned down the hall of the third floor, I saw another teacher fixing her bulletin board. Feeling obligated (because after all I was the new guy), I introduced myself to her. She was a young Latina woman who smiled politely back at me as we exchanged greeting and each other's names. Then came the question:

"So what grade are you teaching?" she asked.

"Oh!" I responded, surprised that she asked. "Third grade. Bilingual."

I could see her rapidly size me up with her eyes. As for my size, let me just say that I could double for an NFL offensive lineman and get away with it.

"Really?... For real? Why not upper grades?" was her response.

This scene would repeat itself quite often, not only in the school building but also with acquaintances and friends. The biggest challenge of being a male early childhood teacher has much to do with false perception and generalized stereotypes of what an early childhood teacher is supposed to look and act. Given some of the circumstances and odds which many teachers must face, I think this challenge is more of an irritation rather than an issue that can impact the breadth and quality of your teaching.

One can assume that the public misconception about the profession of teaching—especially within the early childhood area—is perhaps that women are more naturally adept to work with younger children. According with this perception, women possess a deeper sense of patience and understanding for our younger school aged children. Whereas a man can maybe instruct in the middle or upper school grades where more discipline and structure is needed. These gender biases can—if allowed by the individual—become a construct reality in the practices of teachers. I have heard males colleagues say that they could never work in the primary grades—and also on the other end—female colleagues have cowered over the possibility of having to teach upper grade children. Granted, all have the complete right to express preference in specific grade levels; however, I do not agree with the notion that one gender is either more effective or ineffective to perform as a classroom teacher based strictly on the above criteria. Persistence is needed to work through the assumptions, generalizations and the puzzled stares that male early childhood teachers receive. Keeping focused and being and an integral component in the academic, social, emotional and cognitive development of the children are the key to succeed.

Back to my first day, I opened the door to exit the school building to enter the courtyard where all the children had assembled. I whizzed past neatly lined students packed to the gills with school supplies. Boys and girls, tall and short, skinny and those more like me; blue and white uniforms, many of them worn for the first time. I went into a nostalgic reminiscence, as I walked out to retrieve my students. In my mind, I was remembering my second grade first day of school when I knew that my teacher would be Mrs. Boland. When I met her at the door that day, I felt relieved; she looked so nice. Her voice was like my grandmothers sweet and soothing, her demeanor calm and reassuring. I also remembered my eighth grade teacher Mr. Mooney. He had an ability to always draw out the best out of his students. He listened and gave his students a measure of respect that was in turn reciprocated back to him. I recalled all this and tried to recapture these moments and translate them to the meeting that awaited me. There they stood 26 energetic, eager, and maybe a little bit nervous third grade students. When they saw me their eyes lit up and I heard them say "Maestro," (teacher, literally "master" in Spanish). It is a moment that will have a special place in memory.

Being a male teacher in early childhood education has been a truly rewarding and eye opening experience. I believe that the male presence in the classroom during those crucial early years of schooling brings an added benefit into the social, emotional, and cognitive development of children. I believe that the ultimate success in the journey of life is defined by the quality of our relationships. Relationships with our families, friends, and others are the conduits through which all social inter-action, emotional connections, and cognitive learning are carried through. I can retrace my past and see how positive relationships with my family, teachers, coaches and friends have impacted my life. Equipping our children with the tools to build and develop these relationships is absolutely necessary towards an overall holistic development. When a child has had both male and females teachers in their education, they are allowed opportunities to build relationships with both genders. I posit that this can only serve to enrich student/student and teacher/student relationships. Benefits can then be seen through the social and emotional connections that are being established; hence, the likelihood of cognitive learning is improved.

Being a male teacher gives me the opportunity to help build those relationships with my students and others that I coach or tutor. There is nothing more rewarding than partaking in this with my students. Knowing that bridges have been built and another conduit is open and available for that young person to succeed is very rewarding. These relationships are built through the process of how a teacher operates and manages their classroom. In a classroom that is managed through fear and intimidation, the chance for relationships to grow is restricted. The same would be true in a classroom where the teacher has adopted a dictatorial style. In order to effectively build relationships, the classroom must be an extension of the teacher. There must be unconditional positive regard towards all students, they must feel safe to communicate and exchange ideas and take risks in the various learning activities which take place. They understand that the classroom is now an active learning community. Within the parameters of this community are established principles in place that make the risk that students undertake conducive to the intended learning outcomes. It is through the implementation and creation of this classroom community that meaningful relationships and academic growth are fostered.

It is essential for me to note that these connections do not end with the students but should extend to the parents as well. Having parents on board and in the know with what you are doing in the classroom or on the team strengthens the relationships that are constructed at school. Keeping them informed through newsletters, notes, invitations to attend classroom/school events, meetings or phone calls are vital to strengthening the relationships of students, parents and educators.

At the same time that my experience has been rewarding, it has also been eye opening in regards to the needs of the children living in the inner city. Although there are currently many dedicated male professionals present in the school system, I believe there is a need for more men in the field. The influx of males into the profession could begin to offset the terribly disturbing rates of urban youth (particularly African-American and Latino males) dropping out of school. If these men can possibly seize the opportunities given to them and develop relationship with the students they serve, collectively with parent, community, and administrator support, gains could possibly be made in stemming the flow of inner city youth not completing their high school studies and continuing on to college. The clearest intervention is to meet these students as quickly as possible, and that would be in the early education ages and grades. I would encourage men to step into this vital role, disregard what the misconceptions and preconceived notions may be. The need is present and greater than ever.

My advice to those considering an early elementary career would be to always make a conscious decision and be mindful of the fact that the child's best interest should always be the number one priority. I would also say not to get lost in the numbers game of standardized and the politics behind the bureaucratic system. To paraphrase Einstein, not everything that can be counted counts, and not everything that counts can be counted. Your influence and the relationships that you build with your students, along with an unconditional positive regard towards them, will speak more for your level of work than any test score ever could.

Finally, I think back to that day in September 2001. Through that horrific calamity, amidst of the confusion and questions, was also the beginning of a new path and a sense of hope. Hope that empowers and emboldens the future generations of leaders and policy makers will be tasked to direct the steps of our nation through shadows of adversity. Through meaningful relationships with their students, male teachers can assist in laying bridges and pathways to future success for the children they serve.

FRANCIS WARDLE

9. MEN IN EARLY CHILDHOOD AND NOT APPRECIATED

A Director's Perspective

For as long as I can remember, my father was a teacher. He taught in the small school at Cleeton Court, on the edge of Titterstone Clee Hill, in the beautiful but wild Shropshire countryside in England. He was also the head master, but because it was such a small school, he also taught (and did a variety of other chores, including cleaning out the outhouse). There were other male teachers in the school: I particularly remember Owen, who taught woodwork. We also had many men care for us during Hort (the German word for before-and-after school care). And we had Hort on Saturdays and Sunday mornings. I remember Rudi, Klaus (actually two Klauses), Don, Paul Gerhard and others.

But my favorite male role models growing up were other men in our small, farming community. I would visit Alf and help him collect the hens' eggs; Harry Taylor's carpentry shop with its sweet odor of newly planed wood fascinated me; I enjoyed watching Tommy Paul and Heiner care for our sheep and lamps—using our obedient border collies to round up the sheep in a distant meadow, dipping them in the cold, fresh stream, and shearing off their think coats; and Ulrich and Eric patiently showed me how to care for and harvest all our vegetables and fruits. Later, Roland introduced me to work in our wood factory making toys. Interestingly, I recently talked to a peer from that time, Johnny Mason, who said he believed his most important education was working with the men on the farm.

I was intrigued with the skill and devotion of these men, who, while always working very hard, still had a free moment for us children. Further, these farming activities were far more interesting to me than sitting in a classroom trying to learn academics, which I was not very good at! To this day, I love nature and growing flowers and vegetables in our back yard (and I have threatened to keep laying hens). I also love anything to do with wood and carpentry. For years, I designed and built wooden play equipment for Head Start programs and other programs for young children. I even built a playground in Brazil!

Choosing to Become a Teacher

I initially became a teacher by default. The only thing I really excelled at in school was art (and maybe soccer). Plus, both of my parents were teachers. So I went to

W.Watson and C.S.Woods (eds), Go Where You Belong:
Cultural Workers in the Lives of Children, Families, and Communities, 67–71.

college to become an elementary school art teacher. After my student teaching experience of teaching over 1200 students in a suburb of Pittsburgh, by traveling from school to school with what ended up being a dog-and-pony show, I knew I did not want to teach art as a career. Following my graduation in 1970, I taught for two years in a free school in Taos, New Mexico, when Taos was the center of the counter culture. Then for three years, I worked at a free school in Kansas City, Missouri. I taught children, 4 to 14 years old, and, because these were free schools, I had my hands in almost everything: math, woodwork, science, art, social studies, literacy and dance. We also did lots of projects, including building our own playgrounds and creating two performing folk-dance groups, and we used the community extensively for our teaching (Wardle, 1978).

After six weeks of earthquakes relief work in the Highlands of Guatemala, I decided to earn a Ph.D. in early childhood education. Subsequently, I became a Head Start education coordinator and then a Head Start Director.

The Needs of Boys

One of the first challenges I faced as a new Head Start director was a disagreement within my teaching staff about the placement of children in their classrooms at the beginning of the school year. The teachers selected their own students, and apparently most of them wanted the girls. I soon addressed this issue with a new policy; however, later that year as the result of a discussion I had with my special needs coordinator, I discovered that in our program we had identified almost twice as many boys as girls with a special or developmental needs. Suddenly, I remembered the argument over student selection, and was curious to know exactly what the gender issues were in my program. So I engaged in an informal action research project. I observed my teachers—all women—in their classrooms and the playground and also took a cursory note of classroom equipment and instructional materials. Among the things I discovered were:
- Most of my teachers clearly preferred to be around the girls rather than the boys;
- In the classrooms, teachers tended to be in the dramatic play area, art area, or doing activities on tables, which is where the girls were. The boys were usually occupied in the block area or playing in the sand and water table;
- Boys preferred to be on the floor; teachers at the tables;
- The dramatic play area was called the housekeeping area;
- The housekeeping area only contained traditional female props: women's hats, women's shoes, women's coats and dresses; an oven, table and chairs, a refrigerator, sinks and a baby's cot. They didn't even have a barbeque!
- We had no woodworking furniture or equipment;
- In our nice, expansive playground, there was no garden for the Head Start children;
- Some of the teachers seemed uncomfortable with boy's active and noisy play (both indoors and outdoors);
- Outdoors the teachers tended to stay in one place, such as by the swings and slides, rather than moving around as the boys did.

These observations led to an article in *Exchange Magazine* (1991) and later *Early Childhood News* (2004) about the unique needs of young boys. Not unexpectedly, these articles produced considerable negative responses from educators and women's advocates who deeply believe it is girls and not boys who are underserved in our early childhood and elementary school programs (Sadker & Sadker, 1994). The observations from my informal study led to many changes in our program, from purchasing woodwork tables and equipment for each classroom, and training teachers on how to do woodwork, to introducing a variety of typically male props in the dramatic play area and increasing male volunteers in the program (Wardle, 2003); nonetheless, it was also very clear to me that our early childhood and elementary education programs reflect a female culture. Ninety-seven percent of the teachers, and almost as many directors, are female (Neugebauer, 1999). These percentages are almost as skewed in elementary schools. Obviously women make wonderful teachers of young children, but the overwhelming population of women in our programs leads to certain approaches to the environment, behaviors, activities and preferred subjects (i.e. in many cases, math and science tend to be short-changed) (Wardle, 2007).

Additionally, in my reading for the child psychology classes that I have taught, I have discovered a small but growing body of knowledge that indicates two interesting phenomena regarding gender and young children:

1) Men provide qualitatively different kinds of experiences and brain stimulation for children (more play, more physical activities, and more fun) (Lamb, 2000; Parke, 1996);
2) Children seek out qualitatively different experiences from men than they do from women. When tired, hungry, or needing to be nurtured, they seek out their mothers; when alert and wanting to play and be entertained, they seek out their fathers (Lamb, 2000; Parke, 1996).

Thus it is clear children need both men and women to maximize their full development. Many of our young children do not have fathers at home; many people believe that one of the things we must do to offset the increasingly poor academic performance of boys in our schools is to hire more male teachers.

Girls Need Men too

Equally important, I believe girls need men in their lives just as much as boys do. Three of my four wonderful children (now grown) are girls; I have a great relationship with each one of them, and enjoyed being very involved in their schoolwork and other childhood activities, just as I did with my son. A girl's healthy relationship with a man while she is young develops in her a prototype, which later translates into healthy relationships when she seeks an adult partner of the opposite sex (Berger, 2008). And girls need physical play and other brain stimulation men provide as they grow and learn.

There is considerable discussion in education circles about children and risk factors. These are potential barriers to children being successful in school and later life. Risk factors usually include poverty, disabilities, and minority status. I believe we need to add children growing up without men in their lives (at home and in the school) as having another, significant risk factor. While there is little we can do about homes without fathers, we certainly can—and should—do something about early childhood education and elementary schools without men.

Barriers to Increasing the Number of Men in our Programs

It was one of those bright, blue-sky winter days in Colorado. It was in the late 1980s. I was feeling pretty optimistic. I drove to the state capitol in Denver, parked my car, and entered the room. Bea Romer, wife of then governor Roy Romer, had recently created a public-private early childhood agency named First Impressions. In my capacity as a local Head Start director, I had the opportunity to meet with Bea on several occasions. I told her I was interested in being the first director for this important statewide early childhood initiative. She kindly arranged for me to be interviewed by the state's HR office.

I felt good about my chances. This was the kind of position I had been preparing for. I was a Head Start director; I had earned a Ph.D. in Early Childhood Education, and I had volunteered in local early childhood and infant programs. As a product of early childhood programs myself, I deeply believed in these programs, and in the government's critical role in supporting them; thus, I was keen to demonstrate my knowledge, education, and commitment.

After about one hour, I left the interview in a complete daze. The young, clean-cut interviewer and his secretary were pleasant enough. They asked probing questions and seemed sincere. But the vast majority of the questions had absolutely nothing to do with early childhood education, my qualifications, or my role in early childhood programs. Seventy-five percent of the questions focused on my sexuality, whether I was married, and why a young man with my education would want to work for an agency serving young children. Needless to say, I was not offered the position; the new director was a young woman, as were all other subsequent directors.

Since that fateful day, I continued to work for Head Start also in the capacity as the president of the local directors' association; then I took a job with a national childcare company, headquartered just outside of Denver. But after I left Head Start, I could never get another job in the early childhood field in the Denver area, even though I applied for many. While I had initially assumed the anti-male view of early childhood was isolated to my interview with the State of Colorado, it seems to be an attitude that is pervasive in the early childhood field, at least in Colorado. I now teach at a local community college and for a national, online university. I have also decided to focus my energy, commitment and knowledge on helping poor children in a school in Brazil where my efforts are appreciated.

Real Men in Early Childhood and Elementary Education

My mother and father were both teachers, and so are three of my five siblings. My wife is also a special education teacher; however, we did not encourage any of our four children to become teachers—and so far none have chosen the profession. In today's America, teachers are not respected by politicians and by much of the public.

Politicians who lack any experience in teaching and any understanding of education and learning often control the profession through the use of inappropriate content standards, high-stakes assessments, and other non-educational and non-development policies.

Many reasons are given for the dearth of men in early childhood and elementary education. These include the extremely poor pay and benefits—especially in both private and public early childhood programs (before kindergarten), the fear of child-abuse by parents and administrators, and our culture's belief that women are some-how preprogrammed to be good at caring, nurturing, and teaching young children, and men are not. But the biggest reason, in my experience, is that most women do not want men in the field—at least men with strong opinions. Elementary schools and particularly early childhood programs are a woman's world. They are one of the few fields where a woman is king—ah—queen. And they intend for it to stay that way. Anyone who challenges these values—or is perceived to do so, and is a man—is criticized and ultimately ostracized.

Occasionally, one of my students is a male, and sometimes he will ask me about entering the field of early childhood or elementary education. While this is clearly his choice, I also honestly tell him about my negative history in the field and that I do not support the efforts to increase men in our field because I do no wish other men (and their families) to go through the same kinds of experiences that I have had throughout my career.

REFERENCES

Berger, C. S. (2008). *The developing person. Through childhood and adolescence* (7th ed.). New York: Worth Publishing.

Lamb, M. E. (2000). *Research on father involvement. A historical overview.* In E. H. Peters, G. W. Peterson, S. K. Steinmetz, & R. D. Day (Eds.), *Fatherhood: Research, interventions, and policies* (pp. 23–42). New York: Haworth.

Neugebauer, R. (1999). Recruiting and retaining men in your center. In R. Neugebauer (Ed.), *Inside child care trend report 2000* (pp. 151–154). Redmond, WA: Exchange Press.

Parke, R. D. (1996). *Fatherhood.* Cambridge, MA: Harvard University Press.

Sadker, D., & Sadker, M. (1994). *Failing at fairness: How America's schools cheat girls.* New York: Charles Scribner.

Wardle, F. (1978). *PACERS Model.* Urbana, IL: ERIC Clearinghouse for Elementary and Early Child-hood Education.

Wardle, F. (1991, May/June). Are we short-changing boys? *Child Care Information Exchange,* 48–51.

Wardle, F. (2003). *Introduction to early childhood education: A multidimensional approach to child-centered care and learning.* Boston: Allyn and Bacon.

Wardle, F. (2004, Jan/Feb). The challenge of boys in our early childhood programs. *Early Childhood News,* 16–21.

Wardle, F. (2007, March/April). Math in early childhood. *Child Care Information Exchange.*

Wardle, F. (2009). *Escola Estrela do Mar: A unique early education model.* Retrieved March 18, 2010, from http://www.communityplaythings.com/ resources/articles/curricula/ EscolaEstrela.html

ROBERT GUNDLING

10. A NATURAL INSTINCT FOR TEACHING CHILDREN

Throughout my career as an early childhood professional, I have always viewed experiences through the lens of the children I have had the honor and privilege of serving; therefore, it seems natural to share my thoughts and perception of my role and influence in the lives of the children I served.

From the time I was about six years old, I instinctively knew that my purpose in life was to teach. As I would teach friends in the neighborhood and my siblings, I felt at ease and enjoyed myself. I was learning, the other person was learning, and I was having fun! As I matured, these experiences as a child had an impression on me. I vividly recall one of my high school teachers making a point of telling me that he recognized I had a natural talent as a teacher and hoped I would seriously consider pursuing a career as a teacher. This made sense to me and became the beginning of an intentional effort to obtain the education, credentials, and experience that would provide the foundation for my success as a teacher. A natural instinct for teaching and the influence of important adults in my life as I was growing up led me to a career in early childhood education.

While I was in college, I volunteered in nursery schools, a summer Head Start program and other opportunities that provided me with the experience to solidify my belief that my instinct to teach younger children was correct. I enjoyed this experience a great deal learning a great deal from the children and found satisfaction while working with the children. They were so alive, honest, and excited about learning. I spent my junior year of college in Marburg, Germany. Soon after I arrived at the university, a wise student told me that the best way to learn the language was to work in programs with children. So, I volunteered to work in a private kindergarten and a residential home for children with challenging behaviors. These children taught me that when a relationship is created and based on trust and respect, much can be learned in an enjoyable way, including learning a foreign language. The children were patient and understanding of the time I needed to master the language. I was quite amazed to find that in about a month, I was able to carry on conversations in German with adults with ease.

After graduating from college, I had the good fortune of an offer to teach kindergarten in a suburban school system. I was told that I was the first male hired to teach kindergarten in a public school in the area and possibly the state. There were other men teaching kindergarten at that time; however, they started their career in

W.Watson and C.S.Woods (eds), Go Where You Belong:
Cultural Workers in the Lives of Children, Families, and Communities, 73–78.
© 2011 Sense Publishers. All rights reserved.

"acceptable" grades for men and then move to kindergarten. As a young person, I was naïve to parents who had concerns about their children in a classroom with a male teacher. I wondered why there was a standing audience in room during "Back to School Night." Several years later, I realized that the reason for a large crowd was because the adults in the community were curious to see this man hired as their child's kindergarten teacher. Add to this the fact that there was a teacher's strike during my first year of teaching. I was responsible for 100 first grade students. This experience taught me how important it is to communicate honestly with children and provide the structure necessary for them to feel secure and able to interact safely with each other. We survived the strike, and I think the parents were shocked that a man could manage so many children.

During this first year, there were quite a few learning experiences for me. I had a very supportive principal who believed in me and my ability to work with young children. He always made me feel empowered to create and implement a high quality program for the children and the families I served. He made arrangements for a feature article about the male kindergarten teacher in the local newspaper. He cautioned me, prior to the interview, to be very slow and thoughtful about my responses to the reporter's questions because he believe they would interpret whatever I said the way they wanted it to be, not necessarily the message I intended to convey. So, with enthusiasm and some concern, I participated in the interview. The lesson I learned from this experience was how important it is to be thoughtful when talking with others about one's work.

As the years passed, I had the opportunity to team teach with a female colleague. She shared my philosophy and beliefs about how young children learn. I believe the children thrived because of our ability to work so well together. This served as the foundation for my belief that it is not significant whether the teacher is a man or women; it is more important that the teacher understands and respects the young children and is committed to providing the best environment possible for the child to grow and develop as a successful human being.

During my second year of teaching, I realized, with the help of a trusted and respected colleague, how important it was to support the social and emotional development of a child and a family. Consequently, I enrolled in an Elementary School Guidance Counselor master's degree program. This opened up the door to my discovery of the influence I had on the growth and development of the children. I found that children who did not have a strong, stable male figure in their lives, benefitted from our work in collaboration. I believe a parent said it best, when she told me that she felt her daughter handled the separation and divorce of the couple well because I was a stable male figure in her life at that time. This conversation heightened my awareness of the potential impact I could have on the growth and development of young children.

My experience is that a stable, educated, compassionate male in the life of a child is especially beneficial to boys. I found that boys looked to me as a role model and that positive social interactions between me and the boys served as a model for the boys to follow—and sometimes they followed. I can recall an experience where this was evident during a summer when I worked in a farm in Israel. The family who owned the farm had a son and a daughter. I shared a room with the children and unknown to me, at the time, the son imitated some of my behaviors. I found out about this when I was getting ready to leave their home to return to the United States.

When I think about individuals who served as a role model for me, there are a number of people who come to mind. My father and grandfather are at the top of the list, with at least one male teacher to follow. I realize that as a young child, I was observant of my interactions with these people and the effect it had on me. Most of the interactions were positive and provided me with the realization that if I passed these behaviors and traits on to others, then I would fulfill my purpose in life and make a contribution to society. Individuals who work with children, especially from birth to three years old, impact the cognitive development of that child. As the young child's brain is being wired, I believe what the child sees, feels, and hears influences that play a role in the children's development; hence, men are sometimes less emotional than women and more to the point when addressing a challenge or an issue. For example, I found that children who I worked with seemed to respond well to my straightforward, honest, and caring ways. I believe it was helpful to some of the children as they found their way to process information.

The best thing about being a male teacher is the potential opportunity to have a significant impact on the lives of the children and families who one serves. When a man discovers, as I did, that my purpose in life is to make a positive difference in the lives of children and families, the journey is rewarding, rich, and filled with experiences that are very satisfying. I recall the sense of wonder and amazement I felt the first time I experienced the moment when a kindergarten child "cracked the code" and declared, "I know how to read." My initial reaction was to ask the child how they were able to read the words I was writing on the blackboard. In the spirit of the true innocence of a child, the child responded, "I just do it." When pressed for a more in depth explanation, the response was simple and direct, "I don't know, I just know how." I realized that sometimes it not as important to find out the why; rather, it is a time for celebrating the significant milestone in the life of a child. I realized that the world opened up for this child the moment he was able to read a book; however, the joy and benefit of this experience did not stop there. I was intrigued as I observed this child teach other children how to read. It was during these observations when I learned how she learned to read. I also learned how one person went about sharing their talents and abilities with another person—teaching.

My career progressed with a strong desire to serve children and families in larger cities. I eventually responded to this challenge when I accepted an employment opportunity to work with children and families at the YMCA Child Care Centers in Philadelphia. This experience opened my understanding for the warmth and ease that I noticed in all of my work to date in programs serving children living in large cities. I found that various children in cities did not have a significant male in their lives; therefore, they seemed to look forward to the times that I spent with them. While there were times when their behavior was challenging, they were very responsive to rules we created together for learning. I found that my education in counseling was very helpful in determining if and when a children and their family needed support from appropriate community agencies.

My undergraduate degree is in elementary education and after about four years of teaching kindergarten and first grade, I realized that there was a large body of knowledge still to discover, specifically dealing with the growth and development of children and the field of early childhood education. This led to my decision to pursue a Doctor of Education degree. I would recommend this path to any male who wants to do the very best they can for the children, families, and colleagues they serve during their career. My doctoral program transformed my ability to understand and effectively interact with young children. I made significant progress in knowing and understanding more of the why children act as they do as they experience life during the early years. I also found a new sense of confidence with some of the techniques and actions I learned from my experience with children as the research provided the verification of the value of these behaviors and techniques. This was very important, especially in those situations where my colleagues were mainly women.

An as adjunct professor at several post secondary institutions and an Early Childhood Advisor at the Pennsylvania Department of Education, I had the opportunity to work with first year teachers. Of course, this included men who were considering or who had decided to pursue a career in early childhood education. I have found that what the young men wanted most was the reassurance that their decision to work with young children was "okay." They are also concerned about how to deal with challenges they either heard or believed would face them as they began their career. My hope was that their concerns would decrease as the years passed. Unfortunately, I found that is not the case. Today some men who decide to work in programs that serve young children face the same challenges I faced over thirty years ago when I entered the field. These challenges include reactions from women who, for a variety of reasons, feel threatened by a strong, stable male in the life of their child. In addition, lower status and wages is a challenge for male teachers in comparison to men in other careers. Although slow, however, there has been some progress. Ultimately, my advice to young men beginning their first year of teaching would be to find a strong support system and persevere because of who you are and what you can contribute to others, especially the children. Always remember what matters most—making a difference in the lives of the children.

Larger cities offer the opportunity to participate, in a meaningful way, in breaking the often common cycle of poverty and violence. In my current position as an administrator with a child development program in Washington, DC, located in an area where violence and stress is evident, I often think of the children I interact with everyday as the children of hope. I believe these children have the potential to be leaders in their community and achieve great things, including becoming the President of the United States.

I found the best technique for managing the classroom is to initially create a basic environment for children to learn and then enhance that environment by collaborating with children to create some basic rules. The basic environment includes: a routine for the day, four or five rules worded in what is expected, rather than what is not expected, enough materials and supplies to begin the journey to support the growth and development of the children and plenty of patience and perseverance to make the classroom an environment where a community of learners are focused on creating an environment that supports the children's social, cognitive, and physical development. It is very important to take time to observe young children in action and work with them to create areas where their interests are represented and where they can learn more about what interest them. Learn with them, instead of learning for them.

In addition, with the understanding of how young children grow and development, comes a respect and sensitivity to the rhythm of each child. While children share similar traits, each of them is unique. Working with the child to understand and nurture their uniqueness, helps children feel valued, respected and secure in the environment where they discover themselves. It is also wise to add moments when children are asked open ended questions in order to create an environment where children feel adults listen to them, care about them and sincerely want to connect with them; this is an essential ingredient to the recipe for the success of the child's psychosocial development.

Parents are the first and most important teachers in the lives of the children. Early childhood professionals are expected to create and maintain strong relationships with families. As with the children, what is critically important is to respect and trust the significant adults in the lives of the children and refrain from judging these adults; however, it is important to establish a relationship based on mutual respect. A good place to start in the process of creating a strong, respectful relationship with families is to invite parents and other significant adults in the lives of the children to become active participants in the educational process. This includes an open door policy; actively recruiting family members as volunteers; empowering parents to be involved in appropriate activities and projects that provide opportunities to interact with their child in an appropriate way; create opportunities to support children's healthy growth, development, and success. As with children, the guiding principle should be to work "with" rather than "for" the parents.

Clear communications contribute to strong relationships with families. A clear, concise parent handbook goes a long way to setting appropriate boundaries to guide the relationship between the family members and the professionals. The teachers need to know that the administrators are supportive of their efforts to enforce rules and hold families accountable for the education of their children and program standards. This includes making sure children arrive on time and support teachers when they hold the children accountable for behaviors that contribute to the child's growth as a productive member of society. Finally, there is nothing a parent values more than knowing that the professional staff care about their child and are committed to supporting the emotional, cognitive and physical development of their child while doing everything possible to make sure children succeed in school and life.

I think the most important epiphany during my career came when I was working with a delightful boy who had some challenging behaviors. One day, I started to really listen to what he was saying to me and realized he was doing the best he could and needed me to help him figure out how to learn in spite of his challenges. I realized that as I was actively listened, he was giving me valuable clues as to how he thought and how he was struggling to learn. Together we found the way to help him learn and feel more successful in school. It was important to realize that students

77

have something to contribute in order to better understanding how they learn and what are their needs to thrive in a learning environment, rather than merely surviving.

When I think about advice I would share with a young man considering a career in early care and education, I would suggest that he thinks about appropriate interactions with young children he has had. My experience is that throughout my career there have been those who were suspicious of men who choose to work with young children and question their competency, masculinity, and motives. This has included women threatened by a man who is able to successfully create and sustain strong relationships with children; also fathers who felt they lost their explanation that men do not interact with children since this is the role of women and only those who choose alternate lifestyles enter this profession.

It is important to think these ideas through because of the necessary focus on the safety and well-being of young children. It seems to me this is especially apparent in cases where an allegation of child abuse is reported to a government agency with the responsibility to investigate these allegations. As with any experience in life, there are benefits and there are challenges. I believe the challenge for a man who wants to work with young children, is to build a quality relationship with the children that reflects cultural values and the expectations of others. I found that being cautious of how I interact with the children is helpful to projecting a professional image. During my career, this has meant talking with children, physical contact that is neutral and limited, and showing respect for children. This means learning how to facilitate rich conversations with the children and knowing how to appropriate respond to a child's challenging behaviors.

I believe there are many miles we have to travel before we realize the greatest value of men in the lives of children. Yet, much has been achieved during the past 30 years. With courage, persistence and a clear sense of purpose, young men can find success and rewards in a career as an early childhood educator.

TERRY BUSSEY

11. MY EXPERIENCES IN THE LIVES OF CHILDREN

I have the best job in the world. I fell into a summer position at a childcare center 27 years ago. It was my first real job. At the time, it was just a summer job. Although it was never my plan at the time, it has become my life's work. The work has been challenging, rewarding, and inspirational. I have been a front-line staff member, a supervisor, and a director. I have seen my "kids" grow up, return to work with me as staff members, and even have children of their own under my care. I have seen them succeed and fail and often I have been there to help them find their way. Out of all the many aspects of my work, the things which have easily meant the most to me and have impacted my life in the most profound ways have been what I have learned through my interactions and adventures with children.

My work has not been without challenges. One particular challenge is the fact that I am a male. My work environment is a challenge because I have chosen to work in a field that is dominated by women and is often viewed as the work of females. I have grown to love and respect female teachers over the years. In order to work successfully in this field, you must develop an appreciation and respect for women. Another important discovery is that I have come to realize that children need men in their lives as much as they need women. Many of my experiences over the years have been with children who lack significant male role models in their lives; this makes my work even more important. It appears that over the years, I have had the unavoidable gift of filling the void left by absent or uninterested fathers in their children's lives. This seems to be one of the roles we assume as male caregivers.

There is also a very real stigma that a man who chooses to work with children does so because of some deviant reason. This is a sad fact and probably exists because of the mistakes of a few and the way society has come to view concepts of manhood. Whatever the reasons, we must deal with it as male educators. Some deal with it by choosing other career paths. Others work somewhat in fear, and probably don't give as much of themselves to their work as they could or should if these stigmas were not present. I believe if you are serious enough and have enough passion for your work, you will find ways to overcome these often unwarranted fears as you form relationships, build trust, and rely on your coworkers. There are no easy answers here. All I can say with certainty is that this is what I do; I have a passion for it and I find ways to make it work. I do think that the more good men we have working as educators, the more likely we are to dispel some of these myths.

Another challenge I have faced over the years involves the depth and seriousness of the relationships with the children I work with. I have a great passion for my

W.Watson and C.S.Woods (eds), Go Where You Belong:
Cultural Workers in the Lives of Children, Families, and Communities, 79–82.

work and so this has often led to close involvement with children and families beyond the confines of my workplace. I make no apologies for this when I see a child or a family in need; I do what I can to help. I firmly believe that I am not only an early childhood educator but also a mentor, which is a responsibility I take quite seriously. I have had some interesting dialogue and experiences over the years with parents, particularly fathers, who feel somewhat threatened by my relationship with their children and the perception that their kids listen to me and respect me more than they do to them. Ultimately, what matters is to maintain a good relationship with parents and keep the lines of communication open. We really are in this together, and when you have the best interests of the children at heart, your work sometimes takes unexpected and surprising turns. My experiences in this area have almost always ended up being positive experiences.

If you are a male considering entering this field of work there are a couple of things you should know. First, you must enter this field of work with an open mind and be prepared to grow, learn, and stretch your imagination. This is a career that can take you through many places, but only if you remain open to new ideas and concepts. Children do not fit neatly into boxes and neither should our thinking about them. Secondly, you must accept that this is not a career path that will lead to untold riches or great fame. Professionals should be paid according to the importance of our work; unfortunately, is not the world we live in today. But the work has its own rewards and the longer you do it, the more you will discover about your craft and yourself. We actually do become famous in the minds and hearts of the children we work with. I stand firmly by my belief that helping children become responsible and tolerant adults is one of the most important jobs in the world—and that goes way beyond fame and fortune.

As men, I think we can offer something to children that women may not. I'm not exactly sure what it is, but it is different and certainly no less or more important than what women bring. I speak from my experience with many children who lack a consistent male figure in their lives. Some of these kids, boys in particular, grow up seeing a life of crime as a realistic option. A social worker I know calls them "the lost boys." I call them kids who never had the chance to be kids and experience a real childhood; kids who have been failed in some way; therefore, I have come to see my job as one that shows kids love, support, and acceptance. I also think that as a man, I am able to show boys that growing into responsible men with a respect for women is a good thing. It is challenging work sometimes, but I continue to grow and learn as much as the kids in my care.

There have been a couple of defining moments in my career; things that have reminded with me and have helped me to recognize the value of working with children. A few years ago, I received a letter from a 12-year-old boy at the time who I have known and worked with for a few years. He had some problems in his life and not the least of which was an alcoholic father who could be neglectful and abusive at times. The letter was short and simply thanked me for being there for him, for spending time with him, and for being more of a father to him than his real father. That boy has grown up to be a fine young man with a family of his own. I still stay in touch with him; in fact he was a groomsman at my wedding.

More recently, I quite accidentally came across a note written by a boy who questioned the purpose of his life; he questioned if live was really worth-living and if anyone would really miss him if he was gone. It surprised me as I have known this kid for a number of years and had never had reason to feel he would think this way. But whatever his reason for writing what he did, I had a relationship with him that enabled me to get him some help and show him some very real reasons why his life is important and that he has some great things to live for. Things turned out well. Those of us who work with children have opportunities on a daily basis to encourage them and to make their worlds a better place. It was a reminder to me about the importance of my relationships with the children in my care.

I can't really tell you what the best way is to teach and direct children. Sometimes different things work for different situations. I can tell you what works for me. I would like to think that after 27 years of working with kids, I have learned a thing or two. So here are a few things that I have experienced success with over the years.

First, it is important to like children. That may sound simple and obvious, but your experiences with children will be greatly diminished if you do not truly enjoy and appreciate them and recognize what makes them special and unique. Sometimes it means learning to understand their differences, their challenges and the reasons why they are the way they are. Kids are much more tuned into us as adults than we give them credit for. I can tell you for a fact that they will know if you are not enjoying your work. That's not to say you can never have a bad day; it's equally important for kids to know that we have those too. What is important is that the children we work with recognize our work with them as more than just a job. They must know that we care about them and genuinely enjoy spending time with them. I have seen how a classroom changes when there is no real relationship between the children and their teachers. It is not healthy.

Second, it is important to touch children. Sadly, we live in a world where good, positive physical contact with children is often missing or even prohibited. Sometimes it is lacking from parents. Sometimes a fear of strangers and abuse puts a negative spin on it. Whatever the reason, we seem to be teaching our children to live in constant fear, to be too safe, that no touching is positive. It is an undeniable fact that children need to be touched. They need a lap to sit on, a piggyback ride, an arm around their shoulder, a hug. Once in a while they need to be tickled, or wrestled with or thrown into a swimming pool. Many kids I know have grown up healthy and strong as a result of the good physical interactions they shared with the adults in their lives. Boys in particular can grow up knowing that it's okay to hug and be hugged and to show emotion and even to cry sometimes.

Third, a good sense of humor is important. We need to lighten up. The world is a serious place, supposedly filled with stress, danger, and fear. A kid's world should not be filled with such things. So we need to be able to laugh, and laugh often; sometimes at kids, sometimes with them, sometimes at ourselves (often at ourselves!). You need to work sometimes to see the humor in a serious situation. It has rescued me many times, and given me a new perspective on my work and helped make others around me comfortable. To my ears, there are few things more exhilarating and liberating than the sounds of children laughing. I equate laughter with freedom, and joyfulness. It makes a classroom a happier place. It makes anywhere a happier place.

I work at a centre that promotes outdoor play and believes in introducing and reconnecting kids to nature. This past summer my kids discovered a creek. It's been there in our neighborhood for a long time and we have walked past it countless times. But for some reason, this summer our kids found it and claimed it as their own. For me, this creek came to represent all that is good, all that I love and cherish and value about my job and about children. It was a special place with water, rocks, trees, thistles, slugs and frogs. Our kids waded barefoot in its cool waters. They climbed the trees along its banks and got a good view of things from overhead. They caught frogs and reluctantly let them go. They floated makeshift boats down its small rapids. They built dams and redirected the current. They worked together and co-operated, splashed around, made jokes about piranha and leeches (I didn't see any). They were children of different ages and abilities, some with special needs, yet the only problems we ever had at the creek was when someone would lose their footing and fall in. The creek kept drawing us back. It was a magical place, a small sanctuary in the middle of a big city, a little world all of its own. Many discoveries were made there that summer. After so many years doing this work, I am still amazed and touched by new experiences like this. Of all the many adventures I have had with kids over the years, this was probably the one that reminded me most of my own childhood—carefree days spent roaming and exploring my own neighborhood.

I can't think of a single thing I would rather do with my life more than providing experiences like this for children. I open the newspaper or turn on the news almost daily and am disturbed and troubled by the stories about children, some as young as 10 or 12 stealing cars, assaulting others, getting caught up in the sordid worlds of drugs and gangs and human trafficking. Kids should never have to live in a world where these things become choices for them. And so if I can, even in some small way, offer them experiences that will direct their lives in more positive directions, give them a sense of who they are and who they have the potential to become, that is my job.

So that's my story, and I guess I'm sticking to it. I love my work—I look forward to it every day. More than anything else my work inspires me. I find as much inspiration in it today as I did 27 years ago. Some days you have to look a little harder for the inspiration, but it's always there. It's in the faces of the children who trust you and depend on you. It's there in the laughter, the wonderment, the discoveries, both big and small that kids make every day. And the most amazing thing is that I get to be a part of all that. It makes me feel young, alive and in touch with the world around me. It reconnects me with my own childhood. They say that children choose to surround themselves with the things they like, things that bring them joy and happiness. I happen to think the world would be a better place if we all learned to do that. I really do have the best job in the world.

LOUI-VICENTE REYES

12. A *TESTIMONIO* OF A LATINO MALE
PROFESSIONAL JOURNEY

This *testimonio* (a Spanish phrase whose closest English equivalent would be a testimonial narratives) (Beverly, 2004, p. ix) is a brief story of my professional career in the context of working with young children—one that has been exciting, challenging, and incredibly rewarding. I have used an adapted the model of Journey Analysis (Lawson, 1999) to add structure to my story. Having thirty-seven years of experience in the field of early care and education, I felt that the Journey Analysis model could assist me in describing the substantial complexity of my professional journey. A major contributor to this professional journey's complexity can be attributed to the intersection between a predominately white-middle class-female profession and that of being a man of color and Latino. i.e. the politics of representation of identity and gender as recognized in the literature of critical pedagogy. My story represents my struggles of finding ways to "fit" in the profession. I used the image of a map to guide me in this reflection as well as in the process of exploring the need for future journeys. Using this metaphor of a journey, I will describe my professional self by focusing on the journey itself as a process rather than on the accomplishments achieved through the years.

The intent of this *testimonio* is to provide men in early care and education a story which can be useful and contribute to their dialogue about their professionalization efforts in the field of early care and education. It would be hard to fully understand my journey as a linear or step-by-step process; consequently, I will be using my voice through this *testimonio* to define my reality and give meaning to my journey. As you read the narrative, please keep in mind the dynamic complexity and holistic nature of any journey. Multiple mini-journeys spawned within the broad journey structure of my professional self development in early care and education over the thirty-seven years of experience in the field. Let's began the journey.

I graduated from high school in 1972 already knowing that I was going to college majoring in business administration. This educational goal was identified for me by my father who was keenly aware of the strengths and weaknesses of all his children. Knowing me as well as he did, he knew that I possessed a natural ability of being people oriented and with a good mind for making things happen. Following my high school graduation, I pondered on my college years ahead. I thought about the idea of majoring in business and if that would really make me happy, and more importantly, if that was what I really wanted as a career. Very early in my professional self road I encountered a detour. The summer prior to my first semester of college, my sister,

W.Watson and C.S.Woods (eds), Go Where You Belong:
Cultural Workers in the Lives of Children, Families, and Communities, 83–89.
© 2011 Sense Publishers. All rights reserved.

who was an educational assistant in a community-based early childhood preschool center, applied for a position in the public schools. She was a successful candidate and was offered the position which she accepted only to find herself in a dilemma; did she really want to leave a job that she loved for one that paid more. She was concerned about the preschool, its staff, children, and families. Her desire was to find someone from the community to take her position that possessed a strong disposition of caring for young children like the one she possessed.

I was with her from the start in her quest of finding a new job and vividly remember the moment when it occurred to her that I would be an excellent choice to take her place as teacher assistant at the preschool she loved. I remember that she told me: "You are so good with young kids; I've seen you around them when you volunteered at the school, and oh, my god how the children love you! I think you would be great for my position; you have to say yes and work at the preschool!" She convinced her supervisor that I would be great fit for the job, then proceeded to convince me that I would love working with young children.

That fall, I started my formal schooling in business by taking my first courses in business administration. The community preschool where I now worked had an a.m. and p.m. session with 25 children each. I managed to work in the afternoon session while going to college in the morning. My sister was right; I loved working with young children. In fact, I liked it so much that whenever my salary was paid, I felt guilty to accept it because I didn't see my work as work (a very different story nowadays).

During this time the preschool had many visits from university professors, consultants in child development, and at that time university education students called "teacher-core" interns. As they conducted observations and interviews with parents, children, and staff, they also discussed with me the work I did with young children; they, too, affirmed what my sister saw in my work with young children. I was told that I was an excellent teacher-assistant by the professionals who provided services and visited the preschool. Parents of the children told me the same during parent conferences and home visits, not to mention the children themselves who told me that they loved me. Being modest, I just brushed it off. The university fall semester ended, and I fared well in my studies. Although I was on a professional self journey in a career in business administration, I began to think about whether the road I was taking was the right one.

The preschool calendar was coming to its semester close and in keeping with the school's tradition, a Christmas program culminated the semester, an event that the rural community valued and was well attended by family members, and their extensions was upon us. The preschool director involved me in the planning and directing of the Christmas program during the prior months of school. This experience allowed me to discover talents of music, dance, and directing that I never knew I had. I enjoyed the challenges in directing the Christmas program with great success. In retrospect, I learned so much as to what young children can and can't do. I learned that making things fun works well to get things done when working with both children and adults. I also learned that I was very good at directing and saw what my father had seen in me; that is, the natural ability to get things done.

Prior to the preschool's Christmas break an unforeseen event happened. The classroom teacher that I assisted had to leave her job position for personal reasons. Soon after the preschool teacher announced her leave, the preschool director discussed with me the possibility of my promotion from assistant teacher to teacher of the afternoon session. I was taken by surprise given that all I had was one semester as a teacher assistant experience. Without hesitation I said "Yes, I would take the teacher position." The job served to further affirm my love and work with young children and their families. Additionally, this decision to become a teacher of young children intersected with my professional journey, one where I had to make a stop and figure out which road to take in relation to my future professional career. That Christmas break from both the university and preschool was miserable for me. I found that my professional journey had come to a rest stop resulting in much frustration, fear, and anxiety. The only positive aspect in this rest stop was the eating of yummy Christmas cookies and baked goods, not to mention the delicious traditional Mexican food of the holidays. Nevertheless, a decision had to be made about which road to take next.

The university and preschool spring semester began, and I continued taking courses in business administration as outlined in my degree plan. I started my new job as teacher in the community preschool and really enjoyed the autonomy that came with the position. I remember the children loving to come to school and their parents telling me: "the children can't wait to come to school." The spring semester went by fast and at the end I came to learn that I like working with preschoolers immensely. Again, I fared well in my university studies in business administration. Summer arrived and all I could do was to think about the preschool, children, parents and what my fall curriculum might look like and decided to continue on a career path in business administration. Then came the fall semester and the preschool enrolled its children for that year. It was during this school semester that my professional self in the context of working with young children encountered a huge bump in the road. I experienced how gender intersected with my work.

More Transitions

The month of October arrived and as usual the teachers of the community based pre-school planned their curriculum together the first week of each month. My colleagues, all of whom were women, planned for wonderful learning experiences for their children. When asked to share some of my learning activities, I shared how I wanted to take the children on a field trip to a cemetery that was two blocks from the pre-school, and how this learning experience would give children opportunities to learn about shapes, history, numbers, and to expand their thinking about death. The teachers were appalled by the idea, and when I asked them to tell me why, they shared their concern regarding how in appropriate this trip would be for young children; however, they couldn't really tell me why. To my surprise, the preschool director approved my curriculum, and I thought to myself "off we go to the cemetery!" After the curriculum meeting and feeling uncomfortable about the incident, mainly because I sensed ridicule and an attitude of marginalization, I proceeded to meet with the preschool director. I asked her what she thought the issue was behind the curriculum planning meeting incident that had emerged. In meeting with her, she gave me a big smile and said, "Men think differently from women, many times. I just think that your coworkers are not use to thinking in different ways. You go and do what you have to do and remember, the children and their parents are the ones to tell you if things are wrong." What I learned from this experience was that gender does inform pre-school curriculum and that there exists a dominant way of curriculum planning that may be oblivious of gender differences.

I implemented the planned curriculum and we went to the cemetery; ultimately, the children loved being there. They were so excited about being outside in the beautiful fall weather that New Mexico offers; they never stopped asking questions and learning several new things. The children's excitement drew many parents to volunteer on the cemetery field trip. What evolved were opportunities to establish stronger working relationship with parents. We discussed topics about how to best talk to children about death and how to help children in the event they were to lose a family member. We discussed topics of religion and whether they should be included into the preschool curriculum. The learning experiment was a great success, and I learned that it was okay to think differently. Again, the fall semester went by fast, and I found myself enjoying and knowing that this was the career choice for me and decided to take a different road in my professional development.

The spring semester arrived, and I encountered an uneven road during spring break. I became aware as to how unhappy I was majoring in business and the painful realization that early childhood education in the mid 70's was not a sought-after profession for men. The major reason being that men's role, at that time, included that of being head of a household. I asked myself, "how would I ever support a family with an early childhood teacher salary?" In addition to this bumpy road, I knew that I would be encountering another detour not far from where I was at the moment.

As I continued my professional journey and prior to taking a different road, I encountered a roadblock: announcing to my father, the family patriarch, about the decision I had made of dropping out of the college of business administration, knowing very well that it would end up in a tough argument. Again, the theme in this professional development roadblock was not only about gender, but also related to my Latino culture and identity. The idea that men are the head of household is a strong message that my culture gives to Latino males. This was compounded by the fact that a son does not go against his father's wishes; the patriarchal aspect of my Latino family. I confronted my father and sure enough, he was very upset at my decision and strongly discouraged me. To bring closure to what would have started to be a never ending argument between me and my father, I agree that I would go one more semester in the college of business and then decide what career I wanted to pursue. I already knew what was going to be my career choice; however, I couldn't let my father down, a "male thing" in retrospect.

That spring went by fast, and I became keenly aware that I loved being a preschool teacher. It was at this juncture of my work with young children that I realized the transformation that had occurred in me. Instead of seeing myself working with young children in the capacity of a teacher, I began to see myself as being a teacher of young children and accepted this role; thus, transcending my culture and gender. I was amazed by the creativity that I possessed and how much learning and fun I was having while positively impacting the lives of young children.

That same semester, I started learning about possible new majors to pursue in college other than business. I looked for programs that would provide me with formal training in early childhood education but the choices were limited. During this pursuit, I came across the school of social work. During the early 70's, early childhood education was not recognized as a "field"; consequently, the school of social work interested me because of my experience working with families at the preschool level. Immediately, I decided to take a turn and get on a new road. I decided to major in social work, all the while not involving my father in the decision even though he was paying for my education. Spring semester ended, and again I fared well in my studies in business administration and enjoyed my job as a teacher of young children. I felt as if I was finally back on an excellent road and an exciting professional self journey not knowing what the next destination would be. Summer arrived and a new program came to the rural community where I lived. The program was Head Start, a half day summer program for preschool children.

There were announcements out recruiting for teachers, teacher assistants, and auxiliary staff. Head Start was a summer program at that time. I applied for the position of parent involvement coordinator based on the fact that I was now majoring in social work and was hired. My primary job function was to create meaningful parental involvement opportunities for parents of children enrolled in Head Start. I thought a great place to start would be by meeting every parent through home visits I visited their homes and established working relationships with the parents. I encourage their participation and involvement in classroom activities, fieldtrips, and health visits to doctors and dentists. I also involved them in decision making parent policy councils.

My work experience with the Head Start program was very gratifying and success-ful. The end of the summer program arrived, and it was during this time that the female executive director of the summer Head Start program asked me if I would be interested in becoming the Director of the Head Start program. She mentioned that she was moving and that her position as Head Start Director would be vacant. She also informed me that the hiring would be an "emergency hire" and at a later date, I would have to apply for the position as per the organization's personal rules and regulations. Again, I could not believe that she would ask me to apply for the position knowing that I only had a summer of experience working with the program; nevertheless, I accepted the position with the condition that I could continue my studies in social work until completion of the program of study by taking professional development leave. She agreed and approved the hire.

In retrospect, all the mentoring in the field of early childhood was from women; men were almost nonexistent in the early days of the field. As Head Start Director, I learned about the organization, financial, management and administration aspects of the Head Start program. I became aware that my experience as a teacher and parent involvement coordinator gave me the necessary background for making informed program decisions. I enjoyed the idea of making decisions that could impact the program and be beneficial to the children and families the program served.

It was about this time in my career journey in early care and education that I began to anticipate a rest stop. One evening, while visiting my parents, I discussed with my father the work I was doing and how much I enjoyed it. He smiled and told me, "I knew you would be good at administration." I smiled back acknowledging what he was really saying to me, that I had made a full circle in my career journey. What I learned at this rest stop was that in back of my mind, the politics gender and identity were playing as background music all the while I was on my professional development journey. I came to realize that I had created a space for me where I could honor my male, Latino upbringing by securing a higher paying job in early education and one that afforded me the opportunities to stay connected with young children. I came to know that it was teaching and being in the classroom that brought me the greatest satisfaction. I also learned an important lesson of how well I navigated the detours and road blocks, caused by the intersection between a predominantly white female profession and the politics of gender and identity. This rest stop offered me the space to reflect, rest, and celebrate which was necessary to get back on the road of my professional development journey.

I continued to work as the Head Start Director for the non-for-profit statewide agency until they offered me a senior administrative position of director of their Children, Youth, and Family programs division for the organization. I committed 27 years of service to the organization. During my tenure, the division grew to be one of the state's largest early childhood delivery systems that included Migrant Head Start, Region VI Head Start, State Child Care, After-school programs, summer nutrition programs, federal research and demonstration projects, and others. During the last five years of my service to the organization, I took a detour and began a master and doctorate program of study in early childhood education. Upon my graduation with a doctorate degree, I retired from the organization and again took another road into academia.

Currently, I teach to aspiring teachers of young children. I am an associate professor in early childhood education at a state university. I chose a state university because of its mission; it is "the people's university" and in my state there is a great need for early childhood formal training. The institution affords me the opportunity to create access to formal training in early childhood education to future teachers. I came to this destination in a very similar way I came to be a teacher of young children. Yet again, a female colleague saw potential in me as a teacher educator. She offered me a course to teach in early childhood education all the while telling me that I would be a "wonderful teacher educator." I taught the course and instantly fell in love teaching teachers to work with young children. Her affirmation planted in my mind a career as a professor in early childhood education. Today, I find myself fortunate to be able to work with early childhood professional women that celebrate the diversity of identity and gender. I believe that I offer our university department a unique perspective to the teacher preparation program, informed not only by my philosophical, theoretical, work experiences but also by my representation of identity and gender. The men in our teacher preparation program are thrilled with the idea of having a male professor who is an early childhood educator, not to mention our female students given that the majority of their professors are women.

Currently, I am mentoring a male-student of color, who is a star player in the university's football team. Issues that we have worked through in his practicum and course works that have emerged from the politics of representation of identity and gender have included: guidance (men of color guide children differently than females); curriculum planning (men of color sometimes come up with far reaching ideas for children's learning informed by gender and identity). We have worked together to see professional and personal growth and anticipating student teaching and graduation come spring. In my most recent conversation with him, he shared with me that he has reached a detour in his career. There is a decision to make; that of continuing in the pathway toward becoming a professional football player, which has been pointed out by his coaching staff and could result in substantial monetary gain and perks or to follow his heart and passion for a career teaching young children. Later, he told me that he has made a decision, to follow his career passion of being a teacher of young children. When I learned about his decision it made me happy because I have traveled a similar road and know the work that went into making a career choice. Ultimately, I know he will endure and be happy while benefiting generation of children to come.

The political intersect of identity, culture, and gender (in my case as a male Latino) is a place that men in early childhood education must understand in order to become successful teachers. They develop the perspective to ask unique questions in order to build alliances that are beneficial to their children and classrooms. It is unfortunate that as men continue to infuse early childhood with their ideas and ways of thinking that it is seen as political, given the fact that early childhood education evolved in the United Sates from values that are predominantly white, female, and middle-class. What I have hoped to accomplish through this *testimonio* was to provide readers with another story from which they can continue a dialogue with others about their own professional journey.

REFERENCES

Beverley J. (2004). *Testimonio: on the politics of truth*. Minneapolis, MN: University of Minnesota Press.
Lawson, H. (1999). Journey analysis: A framework for integrating consultation and evaluation in complex change initiatives. *Journal of Educational and Psychological Consultation, 10*, 145–172.

GEORGE YAMAMOTO

13. FINDING MY PLACE IN THE WORLD

My Journey through Early Childhood Education

I was born in Honolulu, Hawaii on the summer solstice of 1967. Growing up in Hawaii was not always sunshine and paradise, but I'll have to admit most of my childhood was awesome. Aside from the typical challenges of being raised in a single parent home, my upbringing was fairly normal. Like many children, being at school was not necessarily a top priority for me. It is not that I struggled; it is just that I was more interested in just getting by, rather than learning for the sake of knowledge and understanding. In my earlier years, I coasted through both school and life; doing the bare minimum in to order to "get to the next step."

Continuing this trend in college, I decided to major in psychology. I thought it was an interesting subject and had heard from others that it would be an easy degree to attain. I was correct in my assumptions; however, when I eventually graduated from the University of Hawaii (UH), I had absolutely no idea what I was to do next. I began to apply for jobs and soon found out my degree meant nothing without some practical experience. I was very frustrated and didn't know what to do. It was not till I stumbled onto a posting for a Residential Counselor position for Hawaii Job Corps (HJC) that I felt everything falling into place. This was something that I was excited to try, and fortunately for me, my previous three years of experience as a Residential Adviser and Hall Director at UH was enough to get me in the door. At HJC, I began as a Juvenile Counselor in the dorm system supervising and counseling residents. Eventually, when I had gained more on the job experience and seniority, I was promoted to a supervisory position.

Shortly thereafter, I began to have doubts about the work I was doing at HJC, which in turn raised complicated questions about my happiness in the work I was doing. I found myself caught in the classic Catch-22; someone in the middle stage of life and contemplating changing careers. As a person who has worked in only one field for many years, I faced a challenging question: how could I afford to change careers without risking everything I had accomplished up to now? I had good job security, great benefits and a quality retirement package. Furthermore, I had my dream house and a fantastic relationship with my wife. I had to confront a question: "was it really worth risking everything just to feel better about the work I did?"

This question went unanswered for many years. I started feeling depressed about the job I wedged myself into. Coincidentally, Fai, a close friend, had given birth to twin boys who were both colicky. She really needed my help. I was the only one

W.Watson and C.S.Woods (eds), Go Where You Belong:
Cultural Workers in the Lives of Children, Families, and Communities, 91–101.

she knew who was available during the day, since I supervised the night shift, and was unable to go to her family for help. I began going over whenever I had the time or felt I had the extra energy to help out. To be honest, it was really not much fun at first. All I remember was that the boys constantly screaming and crying. All I could do was to take the lesser of two evils by trying to comfort the quieter one. As a result, when I finally got home after helping out, I would be sweaty, stinky, and tired. The weird thing was I felt better leaving their house than I ever did leaving my job. Even though I really did not enjoy it that much initially, I knew my help was greatly appreciated and felt I had accomplished something good.

Eventually, I began to enjoy myself more with the twins and less at work. Things began to change as the twins got older. I really started bonding with them. In addition, a bizarre thing started happening: I began going over to the twins' house almost daily, and my experience with them started to change me as a person. Hanging out and caring for them really made me feel better about myself. Along with learning a ton of stuff about infant care, I found that I had a natural ability with young children. My temperament and personality seemed to be a perfect fit, and I never once felt like I was pretending to be good, I just was. Fai noticed this, and suggested that I consider working in childcare as an option for a new career. At this time, I just laughed and replied "just because I'm good with your kids doesn't mean I'd be a good with other kids." After thinking about it for a while, I realized that she was right. Why not check it the opportunities out there. I figured what could I lose? It couldn't be any worst than any of the dumb ideas that I had over the last few years.

I did some research and found that as long as I obtained a few Early Childhood Education (ECE) credits, along with my psychology degree, I would be able to pull this off. I took a vacation to think over my options and when I returned I was convinced that if I did not get out now, I may never be able to. When I returned to work and checked my remaining vacation days I discovered that if I took the remainder of what I had left, my last day of work at HJC would land on my 35th birthday. I always felt my birthday to be special, so I took it as a sign, one of many to come, and figured if I was going to have the typical midlife crisis it seemed appropriate I quit on that day. So I did the unthinkable after over ten years of working at HJC, I resigned on my birthday. I risked my sanity, my house, and unknowingly even my marriage with my decision.

I took my first real risk and let go of my "go with the flow" mentality that had gotten me through life thus far. I was proactive, rather than passive. I applied at Honolulu Community College (HCC) and obtained a part time nanny position using my knowledge and reputation I built while helping out the twin boys. I knew this was an impulsive move and wanted to be sure I did not make the same mistakes I had made in the past. I didn't want to get stuck in another unsatisfying job I did not like. Furthermore, I figured being a nanny for kids I did not know, as well as taking the introduction Early Childhood Education (ECE) classes would help me to decide if this was where I wanted to be.

I was scared but also excited to re-enter school and start taking care of a new set of children. At first, working with both Josh (2 years old) and Andrew (9 months old) was difficult because I had really never done this sort of thing before on my own.

As I began exploring these dual learning experiences, I started to develop an unintentional *symbiosis* to this process that seemed to work very well for me. I began implementing methods from my ECE classes about environment and routines and began integrating it into what I was doing at home. On the flip side, I used my experiences with the boys to help me understand and validate the theories I was learning in my classes. As a result, I'm sure the reason I did better than I had expected was the mutually beneficial relationship that had evolved between my two experiences. My intention was to not only learn the information but to do my best to understand the intricacies of how the information applied to real life situations.

As a result, I realized for the first time in my life I was actually trying to learn with a purpose. I was eager to improve my childcare skills, and found myself constantly asking questions in all of my classes. I attempted to speak less, especially when I felt that I was starting to dominate the general discussions of the class; however, I found that I was still talking more than anyone else in class (prelude to the future). One of my professors, Leilani Au noticed me *because* I talked so much and was annoying her. She had no choice but to get to know me better. For some strange reason, she saw past my annoyance and offered me a volunteer aide position at Keiki Haouli-HCC's daycare and lab school. This is where I learned how little I knew about center-based infant and toddler care. After working with me for a few of months, Leilani informed me that there would be more opportunities for me if I applied to work in pre-school age range. However, she really felt I was a better "fit" for infant/toddler work. I completed the semester and ended up acing all three of my ECE classes and impressed my professors so much that they all offered to write me letters of recommendation to get me started in my new career.

Although I was confident in how well I did thus far, I knew the hardest part was coming. I had some relatable experience as both a volunteer and a nanny, but knew my lack of center based experience was going to be my biggest obstacle. I was strongly drawn to the 0 to 3 age range but had to be realistic. I applied for any and all positions in elementary education. Over two months I sent out resumes to every education related job I was qualified for and ended up interviewing with half a dozen organizations. The directors seemed impressed that I was trying to get into early education, but unfortunately I was not what they were looking for. At this point, I was becoming really desperate. Fortunately, I got lucky when I sent my resume to a local elementary school. I was automatically hired mainly because of my degree. Regardless, I was just happy to finally have a job somewhere. Unfortunately, I knew working with 1st graders in after school care program was not going to help me get to my dreams in ECE.

As a result, to augment my experience, I began volunteering with Early Head Start (EHS) in the mornings. Volunteering with EHS was great, although I got the usual questioning looks at first since I was a male; acceptance came quickly because of my constant interaction in the infant/toddler classroom. Class sizes were small and intimate, so you really got to know the other teachers and kids quickly. I believe that is why I did not experience too many discriminatory situations with the other female teachers. I was obviously happy to be there, and I felt people really liked working with me. If they had any preconceptions about me, it didn't take me long to dismantle those barriers.

Even though I was definitely beginning to be accepted by other teachers, it was not enough. I found out through an area supervisor that EHS requires six months of *paid* working experience for any of their full time positions. EHS was by far my best opportunity because they had sites statewide and my other options were mostly private daycares with rare openings. Although I was upset and frustrated, I continued to volunteer with EHS because I still loved all of the new friends I have made. I just had the feeling that I was still supposed to be there.

A couple of months passed, and I noticed a posting in the paper for an aide position in a small pre-school that has an infant/toddler unit. I immediately applied at the Early School (ES) and I get the call back while I was working at EHS. ES informed me they are doing interviews that morning, so I did not have time to prepare properly. Fortunately, the teachers at EHS gave me some suggestions, and on the way to the interview, I began going over in my head what they may ask and how I should answer. The closer I got to the ES, the more stress I felt as I realized this may be my last shot to work in 0 to 3. My window of opportunity was closing and this was the *only* infant/toddler posting I had seen in the last 4 months. I knew I needed to approach this interview with a different mind set. I decided to just go straight to the interview with out changing clothes (I was in a t-shirt and shorts). I figured why change into something uncomfortable that did not really reflect who I was or the work I did. Following that line of thought, I realized that answering with prepared answers just didn't seem to work for me, so I just tried to relax and clear my mind.

I actually remember mumbling to myself on the way to the classroom "just be yourself and lighten up." I took a deep breath and walked through front gate. Upon entering the classroom, I knew right off the bat this was going to be different than any of my other interviews. I took my slippers off and was warmly greeted by three teachers all sitting on the floor, and all in t-shirts and shorts. I just remember thinking "I'm so glad I did not change my clothes."

The interview process was free flowing and their questions were about things I was already doing at EHS. They encouraged me to ask questions, so I began asking them about whatever came to mind. Eventually, my questions turned into a discussion of the lack of males in ECE (another sign of the future). I actually enjoyed the interview, I loved how down to earth they all were, and they were genuinely impressed at how dedicated I was to "getting my foot in the door" of a 0 to 3 program. The clincher was when they discussed the pay ($7/hr) and limited hours. I replied that although I would have to quit my current afternoon Aide position ($10+/hr), I would be more than happy to do so for the chance to work in this age group. As I headed to the parking lot, I was not sure if I got the position, but I *knew* they got the real me and that was the best I could do.

Once I got to my truck I realized I'd forgotten to give them one of my documents, so I headed back to the classroom. As I peeked over one of the side walls, I was instantly greeted with a sort of gleeful group squeal; I was a little shocked as they all scrambled together to give me a hug and congratulate me. It seems as though in the two minutes it took me to return from the parking lot, they had all decided to offer me the position right then and there without seeing anyone else. They squealed because they were all trying to figure out if they could stop me before I left the parking lot. As I left, I had this weird feeling of destiny and fate. I wasn't sure what my future held or where I was going in ECE, but I knew this was where I was meant to start.

Unfortunately at this point, I was still far from stabilizing my family's financial situation. I had cashed out all of my retirement along with draining our savings but that was still insufficient. In addition, my mom gave me a substantial amount of money to help keep us afloat for the six mouths, while I found a full-time job. My plan at this point was to hope for an opening anywhere that I was qualified for. Yet again, the problem was the same as it was before. The ES was the *only* infant/toddler postings I have seen since I started looking for a new career. "What could happen if I do not see another opening before my time runs out?" I figured I'd done the best I could up to then, so all I could do was be patient and hope for the best.

During my mornings at EHS, I heard about a new aide position at an EHS site located on a local high school campus. I found out I might be qualified for this position because work experience was not required. Since the site had a lot of young babies who were under a year old, they were having problems caring properly for so many infants with only two teachers. Shortly thereafter, I saw the area supervisor and she mentioned the position. Naturally, I applied for it. When I went to my interview, I knew the philosophy which worked for me the last time I got my position at the ES was not going to work today. First of all, I knew I had to dress properly for this interview, so I wore the appropriate dress shirt, slacks and shoes. Fortunately, I made the right decision because this interview turned out to be pretty formal. However, I was very uncomfortable in my stiff pants and shoes and I'm sure it showed. In addition, I felt overly prepared and was way too nervous. When I walked into the interview room, I'm sure I looked truly uncomfortable. I could not help it; I knew that without a doubt, if I did not get this position my ECE career would be over.

Everything changed when I sat down and looked up at who was on the interview board. One of the interviewers was a teacher I worked with while volunteering. Her name was Tita and she was one of the funniest people I have ever met. When I saw Tita not only did I feel better about my chances, but she made me laugh right away and I instantly felt better. Tita knew me well, and it didn't matter how I answered the pre-selected questions, I knew she would back me up. The interview went very well. I felt I could have done better, but I was honest and happy with what I said. Everyone I knew at EHS was telling me I got the position, including the area supervisor; however, no one could confirm it because the processing and background check usually took months. So, even though I had passed my deadline, I had to wait. It took about three months before my paperwork cleared, and I was officially offered the full-time position. There were no words to describe how I felt at that moment. But after I stopped jumping up and down, I did have a new feeling. I felt really lucky, but I *knew* this was meant to be.

I was visibly upset when I left the ES, but they knew I had no choice. I was so sad about leaving that I decided, no matter what happened after this, as long as our bills are okay, I would never change jobs on the basis of money. It's not that I was not excited to be starting at EHS, but I was already happy at the ES. I promised myself that if I was happy at my new job, I would enjoy it for a while and only move onto something new if I thought I'd be happier. I'd have to keep that promise several times while I was working at EHS.

I started working at the campus EHS and by some strange coincidence I already knew my new partner. I worked for several months with Ivy at Keiki Haouli under Leilani, so we clicked right away. Ivy and I were watched closely by the new parents as we were the replacements for the previous teachers they did not approve of. It was not the easiest situation working with disgruntled teenage parents, but we both did well at earning their trust. Before long we all became really close and in less than one month, I was sure, I loved my new job. It was not completely a smooth ride. There were some doubts from people I did not work with directly. I was the only aide in EHS and the only male, so when they do not need me at the high school daycare, I got passed around to sites all over the island. Like my previous experiences, I broke down barriers quickly and everyone seemed to enjoy working with me.

I got a call from the ES Director, my old partner had to quit and they wanted to offer her position to me. I was shocked they would even consider me. The salary they offered was very competitive for any 0–3 teaching position, and it was more than I was making at EHS. They give me until the end of the week to consider it. I tried to figure out what to do and one morning a little boy named Angel reminded me of the promise I made to myself after I left the ES. I remember the moment well because Ivy took a picture of it unintentionally. Finally, it was the end of the week and I had to decide. I was finger painting with Angel against the front door of the classroom I helped to recreate. It was just me and Angel that day. While Ivy was doing paperwork and I was having the best time playing with Angel, I started tearing up and immediately *knew* why. I did not want to leave and I didn't have too. I had that same comfortingly feeling of destiny and fate that I felt the first time at the ES, and I knew I'd made the right decision. I was offered several other lead positions while at EHS but I decline those as well. My wife gave birth, and I was so happy with my new baby girl Kealani; life was good, and I couldn't see a reason to change anything.

I was impressed with how sure she was about her opinions, but I honestly, at this time, I thought they were a little extreme. She argued against the intentions of family style for the 0–3 and stated that they were inappropriate. Despite what she stated, I still saw positive values in it, so I would not back down with my defense. Deidre was so convincing I had to ask her "okay, if you're right, what can we do, these procedures are written in stone." Her response was: "you could refuse to do it, and if you all banded together, you could convince your supervisor to change policy." This is an example of what I thought it was Deidre's extreme side. I guess I also made an impression because after the class she approached me and said, "Mister George, did I scare you?" I was caught off guard, so I lied (she did scare me). I said "No; that was a good discussion."

I completed the West-Ed series with her and despite her occasional passionate outburst I loved the way she described early childhood, especially because she was strictly talking about 0–3 yrs during West-Ed trainings. She kept constantly reminding us of the difference between expectations of preschool and infant/toddler. Her style reminded me of Leilani Au's and even though she could be intense, I could not help it, I absorbed everything she said. Her trainings provided me with more than applicable theories but also helped me to organize the framework of my own opinions. Eventually, I started having more opinions about the procedures I was mandated to follow.

At the end of my second year with EHS, the two new teachers I just started with suddenly ended up leaving. I'm uncomfortable about going through another transition after a tough year of changes and I'm wondering if this is another "sign." Although I was happy at this time, I wondered if I was going to feel the same way next year. So one Sunday, I decided to look through the paper just to justify to myself that I was in the right job. I was sure that EHS was the best option I had in the 0–3 center based care; everyone had told me that from the beginning. There were other private schools with great reputations and paid very well but most of them start at the pre-school level and were extremely difficult to get in. Without a doubt, the school with the best reputation as far as pay and work conditions was Kamehameha Schools (KS). I never really looked too closely at KS postings because I knew I would never be qualified (because I thought they only had preschools). However, unbelievably there was an infant/toddler posting for a teaching assistant. My first thought was, "wait a minute, did KS have an infant/toddler program?" After some research, I found out they just started a pilot program less than a year ago, and their site was located in Waimanalo, just 15 minutes from my house. I had to go for it; it was too good of an opportunity, and I always wanted to work in my own community.

As I looked through the extensive online application, I started to formulate how I want to answer the essay questions. I started busting out books, handouts, etc. I began to overanalyze what I thought I should say and basically start stressing out about the impression I might make with the wrong information. I recognized this feeling; I was trying too hard again. I quickly dumped all the books and papers off of my table and literally wrote off the top of my head. If they hired me and it was meant to be, then I wanted it to be on the basis my words not someone else's. Because if this was where I am supposed to go, then I wanted to be sure they hired me for the right reasons. Whether it was work conditions or administrative support, I assumed there was something special about Kamehameha Schools which had nothing to do with how much money they had. Most of my educational opinions I mentioned in my application were based on Deidre's West-Ed training. It was the only ECE information I could spit out straight out of my head with any real conviction. The application was accepted, and they scheduled the interview two weeks later.

The interview consisted of a three person panel on a long table (I was hoping for the floor again) and started very formally. I showed up in a t-shirt and shorts; I knew I should had explained the way I was dressed, but I was more worried about throwing up in front of everyone. The very first question was about the Kamehameha Schools mission statement. Since I refused to prepare, I told them I didn't memorize it and asked them to move on to the next question. Undaunted, I continued on my mission to say exactly how I felt no matter how it would affect my hire. It was actually pretty fun once I stopped taking it so seriously. They asked me what I considered to be my greatest accomplishment/achievement, and that was simple, I said "my daughter

Kealani." It probably would have been better if I talked about my ECE experiences but my daughter was my true answer. I admitted that I did not take criticism well, especially from people I did not work with directly. I even mentioned that if they expected me to teach numbers or the alphabet in an infant/toddler class that they should probably hire someone else. I also had the opportunity to discuss many of my strong opinions about 0–3 work; most if it was based on the ECE based philosophies I discussed came straight out of Deidre's mouth and the West-Ed training I took. I may have been a little too honest, but I could tell I did well because even though we were done, they were still asking me questions. I leave them laughing as I mentioned how close they all were to seeing me throw up. I headed home, and I have the wonderfully satisfying feeling that I have done it again. Not that I had done well as with the other interview, but that I did well in representing myself. I was sure if it was meant to be, they will hire me.

Less than a week later, I was called by KS and despite the fact I was the first person to *ever* showed up in a t-shirt and shorts, I was offered the position, which I graciously accepted. It was difficult leaving EHS, but the more I learn about how cutting edge the Hi'ilani Program was, the more exited I was about being with KS. On my first day of orientation, I had two surprises that "sweeten the pot." The first person I meet was Kaleo Puana, a child development specialist. He was the first male teacher I got the opportunity to work with in the 0–3 and instinctually I know this was going to mean something. My second surprise totally cached me off guard; the curriculum director for this new innovative program was Deidre Harris (no wonder I did well in the interview). After we stopped laughing, Deidre and Shelly Aiona, the Program Director, described the basics of this new program. The philosophy and intentions mirrored my own personal opinions about 0–3 (age specific classes, focus on process, learning through play, etc.). However, I believe what was the most exciting part to me was how much of an influence we would have on this program developed. We were the pilot site; there were no models for us to follow. We were going to be trained and guided but the rest would really be up to us as a three person team. The possibilities as for what we could do were almost limitless. The program has progressed quite far in the last 3 years but the possibilities are still the most exciting thing about this job.

It has not been an easy road for me through ECE but there isn't a single day that passes where I do not have some sort of realization of how lucky I am. My job and my life are no longer separated but flow together enhancing each other. I look forward to going to work as much as going home. I've called this my dream job, but it really isn't. I've never dreamed of anything like this. What I have now is way beyond my dreams because I never imagined anything with this much potential. I love my job with KS and will probably never leave. However, if I do decide to try something different, I feel, I now have *many* options in teaching, parent education, and maybe even father involvement. I am not sure what my future holds, but I will never forget how I found my place in the world.

My advice to anyone trying to get into ECE is to try some volunteering before you commit too much to any age group. That is one of the benefits of my varied experiences at mid life; I unintentionally got to work with almost every age group.

Because of those experiences, I am more confident than ever. Leilani was right when she thought I'd be better with infants and toddlers. I cannot predict anyone's longevity in ECE, but I can tell that you if you struggle with a certain age group, you will probably know if fairly quickly.

For men entering ECE, it may be challenging at first, but eventually it will be worth it. One day when we were having a meeting at the ES, one of the teachers Malia told me "You know, after a couple of years, you're going to be quite a commodity." I remember thinking, "What are you talking about?" And now I know. Breaking down teaching barriers in ECE is not easy for men, so if the transition does not go well, a lot of men do not stick around. However, those that do survive the challenges reap the rewards. When I first started working for EHS, I was constantly complimented by upper management staff. Once, during a federal review, someone actually thanked me for being a man, and I said "Thank you, I like being a man." Back then I was kind of irritated with some of the attention I was getting. However, now I'm a male advocate. Now I understand why they were saying those things. First, I thought they were complementing me because I was a man in women dominated field, but I'm sure the reason they thanked me was because they knew it was not easy for me to get to where I was.

In 2008, I attended the World Forum-Men in Early Childhood Education held in Honolulu, Hawaii to show support for men working in ECE, but I knew nothing about these issues other than my own experiences. I have always been a father involvement advocate because of my own personal experiences and the experiences of the families that I have worked with. But I was still a relative beginner in the field; what did I know about getting more men in ECE? However, what I discovered was father and teacher involvement in early childhood was strongly linked. After talking with a lot of different "movers and shakers" in ECE such as Francis Carlson, I found another inherently "symbiotic" relationship between father involvement and men in ECE. The issues for both topics seemed linked because they are both based on societal preconceptions of men's involvement in early childhood. The classes we are teaching at Hi'ilani are definitely changing outdated pre-conceptions for our families. Hopefully with time we can have some overall effect on how our community thinks about men and young children. Change will undoubtedly come slowly, but if we can have some affect in male involvement in both the home *and* the schools maybe we can change the world a little.

I know I was meant to work in 0–3, but I was also meant to be a role model to other males. And I do not mean it in a superior way, just because I have knowledge and experience does not mean I apply it better than any other male practitioners do. In the real world, I am like every other dad; I try to do the "right" thing as often as I can; however, in class, and in any situation where someone asks for my opinion, I do have a responsibility to model and discuss why male influences are important for well rounded development because I personally know why it is important. Furthermore, the research is undisputable and the studies are endless. Yet, the studies about the effects and lack of male involvement just fail to engage me. What influenced my opinions was what I experienced, not what I read. Growing up in a household with an absent or non-existent father was the norm when I grew up. And later in life, no matter where I worked, or where I hung out at, if I was playing with young children, I rarely saw another male. I believe what motivates men to be more involved with young children is seeing others males do it more often. I believe that is the best thing about being a male teacher, it's not the attention you get, but how big of an influence you are by just being there. Kaleo and I have a *huge* impact on all the kids, the parents, immediate family, and even the extended families. I know before we met, Kaleo and I were breaking down teaching barriers in ECE, but now as team we are breaking down barriers in other places.

If you want to break down barriers with parents, one of your best opportunities is working with families in 0–3. In this age group, you really have an opportunity to get to know your families well enough to "go deep" and really help them with some of their childcare concerns. In any class, a lot of mutual communication between teacher and parent is required for your experience to be truly beneficial for the child. So take advantage of the intimacy of an infant/toddler class to get to know your parents as well as you know their children.

My two main role models through ECE were definitely Leilani Au and Deidre Harris. Leilani became my first role model in ECE because she showed me teaching did not have to be bland or pre-packaged. She did not lecture in her class she just talked and it was the way she spoke about infant/toddler work which drew me into that age group. It was no accident meeting her. If Leilani is responsible for where I came from in ECE, then I can thank Deidre for where I think I'm going. My initial impression of Deidre has not changed much since the first time she tried to get me to "rally" against family style serving. As I mentioned before, at the time I thought her suggestions were extreme and unrealistic, but you know what, she was right. Some of my opinions are so strong now because I can back them up with knowledge and experience. I thought about it recently, and if I went back to daycare and was asked to serve family style, I would refuse and I'm fairly confident I could convince any supervisor I am right.

I have this silly bumper sticker on my truck that says "Men that change diapers, change the world." I cannot tell you how many dads I have seen slapped by their spouses because they were driving behind my car and had no choice but to read my bumper sticker. I have also seen a lot of laughing and hugging as a result of the bumper sticker. Imagine how many men you could save from a slap if you just showed them how easy it is to change a diaper. I'm sure if men knew they would get "something" more than a hug if they *shared* the responsibility of childcare, I know every guy would be trying to do it more often.

Working with young children changed me. It made me more aware of qualities I always had, but never appreciated. I've always been sensitive and nurturing, raised by a single mom; my brother and I were both like that as kids. But as I got older, I think I tried too hard to "fit" into the mold of the stereotypical man. I am not a tough guy; in fact I'm totally the opposite of that. But since I have been working in ECE, I have a better understanding of why am different and that's why I am so passionate. Now I am proud of the qualities I have that make me seem different. I was meant to be here in ECE because I know it is my responsibility to be myself and play the "role" as born to do. Growing up and into adulthood I played too many "roles" that were in conflict with my real temperament and personality. There were many "signs" I should have seen about the person I was meant to be.

Since some of these "signs" seemed like they could have just been coincidence but now after reanalyzing them, I feel "someone" has been trying to tell me something for quite a while. I have never been a particularly religious person but the luck I've had in ECE defies the percentages. The people I happen to meet just could not have been a coincidence. But now I *know* it wasn't; everything "fits" too well for it to be an accident. I'm not going to start preaching about "divine guidance," but I do have a different perspective about God now. I am now sure what my experience will mean to others, but I know what is has meant to me. I do not know who I owe (besides my wife) for what I have, but I know I owe someone. The great thing about paying back this debit is the knowledge that I do not have to do anything, just relax and be myself.

BRUCE S. SHEPPARD

14. A LIFE'S JOURNEY IN THE LIVES OF CHILDREN

My father was a research scientist and my mother started college when I was 4 years old in 1955, studying to be a kindergarten teacher. In 1959, the local school district asked her to teach kindergarten before she finished her degree. She took the position and continued college part time, graduating with a B.A. the same year I graduated from high school in 1970. I mention this because I figured out many years later that this effort by my mother influenced me in two important ways: first, I realized that teaching young children was a valuable work; second, I understood that going to college as an adult was a good thing to do.

I went to seminary after graduating from college in 1974. My first term there was a 10 week field experience in a Head Start program. Working with the children and teachers in Head Start was the most fun I had enjoyed in my early life. I finished seminary in 1979, but within two years, I was ready to quit church work. I remembered that great Head Start experience and found a job in a day care in Minneapolis at the Glendale Child Development Center, directed at the time by the late Jim Greenman.

Glendale was the perfect place to cut my teeth on an early childhood education (ECE) career as a man. Out of 24 full and part time staff, we always averaged 10 men during the 6 years I was there. During that time, I studied early intervention and early childhood special education (EI/ECSE) at the University of Minnesota, and in 1988, I began to work with EI/ECSE children in the public schools. After stints in Minneapolis, Washington state, and Oregon, I began my present position at the Oregon Department of Education in 2008.

While in Minnesota, I began the Minnesota Men in Childcare group with Bryan Nelson. We conducted numerous workshops and retreats for men in ECE in Minnesota until I moved to Washington in 1993. This program was transformed into MenTeach by Bryan Nelson. In 1992, I co-edited "Men in Child Care and Early Education" with Bryan and was a contributing editor of "Working with Fathers: Methods and Perspectives." Also, in 2001, I worked with Bernard Cesarone at the ERIC Clearinghouse to establish the "Men in ECE" listserv. I continue as the principle moderator of this listserv.

Referring to the biography narrative, I was one of those "accidental" men in ECE, or at least for a while it appeared accidental to me. I had always thought that the Head Start field experience in 1974 started my journey into ECE, but now I am not so sure. With the influence of my mother enjoying teaching kindergarten, and growing up with the family value of treasuring young children, a career in ECE may have seen as a logical path. I always figured I would stay in the classroom forever. I thought that when I reached my 70's, I would still teach ECE part time. A severe bicycle accident in 2005 changed my career path and led me to my present position.

W.Watson and C.S.Woods (eds), Go Where You Belong:
Cultural Workers in the Lives of Children, Families, and Communities, 103–106.
© *2011 Sense Publishers. All rights reserved.*

I had a career goal that maybe in my mid 60's I would find a position or opportunity to pass along my experience and expertise to the next generation of ECE teachers. When I had the accident, which could have been life-threatening, I realized that I couldn't count on living well into my 90's, the way all my relatives had. I took my time and looked for a leadership position where I could support today's ECE teachers. In late 2007, I applied for an EI/ECSE position with the Oregon Department of Education; was selected for the job, and started my new job in March 2008.

In 1976, I began working part time in a church as Director of Christian Education and Youth Ministry while I finished my seminary degree. I received that degree in 1977 and began a similar full time position in a different church. By 1981, I had decided church work was not the career for me. I remembered that great field experience in Head Start a few years before and thought I could give ECE a try. At the time, I figured I might stay just a year or two and move on to something else. Twenty eight years later I am still in the ECE field.

The challenges are mixed from my perspective as a veteran ECE professional. I have never faced major problems such as parents being overtly against me as their child's teacher, job discrimination, or child abuse accusations; however, there have been difficulties with female colleagues over the years. Although those colleagues have been publicly supportive of men working in ECE, I have frequently encountered passive prejudice from them. For instance, I don't get included in the communications loop; I don't get invited out to lunch, let alone to the outside of work social networking; and norms for teacher support, such as official staff gatherings or refreshments at a meeting, have been 100 percent feminine in style. A couple of times I have encountered female colleagues that had their own personal problems with male relationships. In those cases, they projected their fears onto me and worked toward removing me from the work environment or at least to have my authority or responsibilities diminished. Fortunately in both cases, I had female supervisors who understood what was going on and put a stop to it.

I also believe that the rewards and advantages of being a qualified male in ECE have more than outweighed any problems I have encountered. Parent support has been tremendous. I can tell the children really enjoy me as their teacher. When looking for a new job, I have been fortunate in finding places where being a man in ECE makes my resume stand out rather than as a reason to put me to the bottom of the pile. From the earliest days of my career in ECE, the two justifications for having men in ECE I heard most frequently were that boys needed men in ECE for positive male role models and gender equity issue. I still think these are good reasons for our presence in ECE, but I do not think they go nearly far enough.

I believe there are other positive reasons for having men in ECE that especially support children's social development. The positive male role model idea also applies to girls. Not only do they need to see good male characteristics for their own social development; I believe girls need to have a positive experience with a male caregiver (father or teacher) to be able to know a positive male role model when they relate to males in their teen and adult years. In addition, I believe children know that half the population is male. Children seem to have the need to understand that men value them as much as women do. When children get these positive experiences from men in their early years, I believe it has a profound and positive effect on how they see themselves in the world.

I know there have been studies on the effect of men in ECE and children's cognitive development, but I think the cognitive effect is less profound. In my experience, men are more likely to lead children in more active pursuits in the classroom and outdoors. They are also more likely to allow children to take physical risks and experiment with materials. These are elements of learning that are essential to a child's healthy cognitive development. From my own experience, it has seemed to me that the positive effect I had on children's social skills was greater than any effect I had on their cognitive skills.

As I mentioned previously, it took me awhile to understand that my own mother was one of my role models. In my own schooling, I did not encounter a male teacher until 6th grade. I didn't get to play much organized sports as a child. Church education and scouting did not have male leadership until I was eleven years old. My father was a fine person but couldn't figure out how to relate to us well until we became teenagers. I had some good teachers, coaches, and scout leaders in my teen years. I would have to say that a true role model for teaching ECE did not come along until I began to work full time in the field in 1981. My principle role model then was my director, Jim Greenman. Although he was just a few years older than me, he was a good mentor who showed me how a male educator could have an impact in ECE and taught me the possibilities of ECE as a viable and exciting career.

As the years went by, I found support in male colleagues I encountered, especially in Minnesota. I count Bryan Nelson, Steve Weber, Harlan Hanson, and Bruce Cunningham in my first circle of influence. After that, there are too many persons to acknowledge. I believe there is still a tendency in society to view the husband/father as the principle income earner. In my 28 years in the ECE profession, I have had numerous conversations with men who were not enjoying their present career, but felt they had to stick with what they were doing to support their family. Other problems they cited for not changing careers were the lower income, cost of re-training, and the time and effort involved with making a career change. I mention this because once I entered the field of ECE, I have been happy with my work, and never encountered a reason to get out of the field. I have been lucky that I have had work that is rewarding and fulfilling. Something many men cannot say about their careers.

An additional positive thing about being a male teacher is the responses from the children. I can see a "hunger" in how that seem to crave male attention. Just as ECE professionals are now talking about a deficit of physical activity and a deficit of exposure to the outdoors for today's children, I think we should also be talking about a deficit in children's positive interactions with men. I find it rewarding when I can make such a difference with children. My friend Bryan Nelson frequently approaches men working public minimum wage jobs, such as mopping the floors at McDonald's, and starts talking to them about how they could earn just as much or more money by working with young children. I think what Bryan is doing starts with an excellent premise—if the pay is the same or better, why not think about teaching children?

There are many men in the workforce whose primary work ethic is not making as much money as possible. When as a society we do not consider teaching young children as a good career choice for men, we do many men a disservice. As I talk to men about this topic, I ask them to think of ways they could try on a teaching role, such as volunteering or working as a substitute teacher. When men break this barrier and take a chance on this work, many of them find out that ECE is the place for them.

Change is good. Just as in many other fields, ECE and elementary education are evolving. My personal philosophy has been to look ahead for new directions and avenues in ECE to explore. With little fear, I have taken the plunge over and over as I change jobs, cities, and career emphasis. A first year student needs the vision to see how the ECE field is changing now and may change in the future, and use that information to make sure he is ready to respond to those changes as they come along. I know someone has given this technique a name. When things get a little chaotic and too many children have become unfocused in their choices and play, I will bring something out of the storeroom, or change an existing learning center, or even just bring out my guitar and start singing. The idea is to have some of the children focus their attention on something positive I have organized for them. This technique goes a long way towards calming a situation or assisting children in gaining focus, without the need to give orders and commands or instill unnecessary discipline.

I make sure parents understand when I first meet them (and frequently remind them in later meetings) that my classroom is always open to them. I tell them that it would be helpful if a visit was planned, so I can ensure there are not too many adults in the classroom. But I also make sure they understand that they can always drop by any time they want. I think this idea really helps set up the parents as team members with the education of their children. I also tell parents that I see them as the expert on their child. I may know principles of ECE and special education, but they know their own child the best. Often it seems this attitude is like a breath of fresh air for parents. It validates their ideas and feelings and sets up an atmosphere of true dialogue and partnership with their child's education.

Way back in the 80's, when I was a childcare teacher, my wife and I took a trip to Florida. We brought back a suitcase full of sea shells. It did not take long for us to realize we had no good use for most of the shells at home. I decided to bring the shells to school to see what I could do with them with the children. After setting some of the shells out for the children to mess around with, I thought the shells were not being fully used. One day, while the children were in naptime I had a new idea. I buried some of the shells in the sand box outdoors and did not tell the children they were there. After naptime was over and the children had their snack, it was time to go outside. It took about 10 minutes for some of the children to discover this buried treasure. We allowed the children to take home what they found. It was just a lot of fun.

What I realized with this experience was that I could have a lot of fun with the children; I could trust my spontaneous ideas; and that most of my ideas were pretty good. Up until this day, I had looked upon my brief career in ECE as a great adventure of being a man in a career dominated by women. After this experience, I saw myself as a good ECE teacher first and a man in the field second. I still carry this image of myself in my work today.

ROBERT M. CAPUOZZO

15. CALLING MY "MALENESS" INTO QUESTION

Currently, I am an Assistant Professor of Early Childhood Education (ECE) at the University of Alaska Anchorage. I hold three degrees in ECE; I was a classroom teacher for six years in multiple settings and have been a trainer for in-service teachers and child care providers. Over the years, I have supervised student teachers in PK-3rd grade classrooms, conducted research in child care settings, Head Start centers, and public school settings. In addition, I work with fathers and infants as a parent educator. In each of these endeavors my "maleness" was called into question. What follows is an account of my path to the present.

How Did I Get Here?

Growing up in a large family there were always many young cousins at family gatherings. Reflecting back on those days in middle childhood, I can vividly recall playing with the kids. Eventually, I consciously made the decision that I would rather be actively engaging with the young ones rather than sitting around the table with adults and older peers. Most readers understand the powerful feeling of energy one receives when you are around kids. It is real and powerful. I felt this at a young age and was fortunate enough to live in a family that valued male involvement; lived in a community that supported young men and women to work with children at camps or as coaches; and attended a school that provided me the opportunity to visit and assist in elementary school classrooms. Due to these experiences, I was privileged to have the courage to give ECE a chance as an undergraduate but not after first trying another major.

I entered Ohio University and declared my major as health services administration. I realized as a work study student at the university student health center that being an administrator in a health setting wasn't all that fun. While I completely respect health care professionals, I personally did not want to spend the next few decades being around sick people who were generally and rightfully disagreeable. I remember thinking about the bits of advice many persons give me as a young adult, "Do something you like doing," or "Pick a career that you enjoy because you're going to be doing it the rest of your life!" I knew I liked being around children; I'd already been in classrooms, coached my little brother's soccer team, being a camp counselor for kids headed to kindergarten. So, I found my way to Tupper Hall and at the door of Dr. Helen Hagens, a professor in ECE. I told her my story and she listened. I decided to change my major immediately to ECE. She helped me switch my work

W.Watson and C.S.Woods (eds), Go Where You Belong:
Cultural Workers in the Lives of Children, Families, and Communities, 107–112.

study assignment from the health center to the child development center and my career in ECE began.

As soon as I walked into that preschool classroom, I experienced firsthand what a magnet a guy was with young children. Many young children are attracted to men in early childhood settings because they may not have a positive male role model in their everyday lives. But even those children with an involved dad seem to gravitate towards men in ECE settings because we are so rare. ECE settings are full of females; when a young child sees a man walk in the classroom it is an uncommon occurrence and one that deserves some investigation. Do the differences between men and women teachers stop at appearance? Of course there are always exceptions, but I believe that men teachers *are* different than female teachers.

The reasons for these distinctions are more suitable for another narrative but generally have to do with socialization, gender identity, and genetics. I want to be clear that I don't feel men are more effective teachers than women or conversely that women are better than men but that men have something completely different and extremely valuable to offer ECE. Men have the experience and knowledge about growing up as a boy; this is a main argument put forth by scholars as a reason more men are needed in ECE. Men conceivably can better understand boys having been a boy. Women on the other hand better understand girls and often (but not always) find it difficult to meet the needs of boys in their classrooms. Men, in general and in popular depictions, are playful beings who enjoy sports and horsing around (again not to say that women in general dislike this behavior). This behavior matches well with the job description of an ECE teacher and with the energy level needed to be a teacher.

I've had some heated debates with female colleagues about being a man in ECE; specifically, am I a good teacher because I interact with children in appropriate ways and develop and implement developmentally appropriate activities *or* am I considered a good teacher because I am a male? While these two facets of my teacher self are inextricable, it brought about some excellent discussions. I'm not sure I knew how rare men are in ECE are that point but I sure was *the* token male (actually Tim was also in the program and was also a *token*). I loved it from those first days; my job was to play with children; as a playful individual this was right up my alley. Of course, I also sanitized and swept floors and saw what it took to be a qualified teacher.

After I completed my undergraduate degree in ECE, I relocated across the country to Eugene, Oregon. Visiting the National Association for the Education of Young Children (NAEYC) accredited center, I was hired upon first meeting the lead Pre-K teacher at Oak Street Child Development Center (CDC). I immediately realized that this was a difficult, time consuming, physically draining job but rewarding as well. I also recognized that I was now in the real world which barely resembled the lab school where I spent the last three years of my ECE life. I was the only man in a center which employed approximately 15 staff members. While I was received with open-arms from the director of the center, this was not the case from my assistant teacher or the other teachers in the center. I like to refer to this as a "Sink or Swim" test. They may have been wondering, "Who is this guy?" "Why would a guy want to work with young children?" "Who cares if he has a degree in EC, can he really work with children?" It took time, but I built relationships with my co-workers and let my actions speak for themselves. This is an occurrence that many men encounter when entering a new EC setting and one in which pushes men away. It is unfortunate considering the obstacles, both personal and social that men have to hurdle to get to this place and then once they get there their supposed colleagues shun and reject them. This is an unfortunate reality.

After teaching for three years in Pre-K settings, I accepted a position that brought me back to my alma mater and to the lab school where I completed my undergraduate work. It was here that I recognized where my career in ECE was heading. In this position as a master teacher in a preschool classroom, I had the dual responsibility of caring and educating young children and their families as well as educate and supervise pre-service educators whom were completing field experiences in my class-room. While the majority of these pre-service educators were female, I was able to mentor a handful of men who were pursuing a degree in ECE. I saw that I enjoyed working with college students who were studying to be early childhood educators. I entered the master's degree program in ECE and taught a couple of introductory classes at the university. I had a difficult decision to make. As a male in ECE, I was needed in the classroom more so than riding the "glass escalator" to a professorship in ECE. Personally and professionally I decided for myself and my family that I would pursue a doctoral degree in ECE. I told myself that I wouldn't become one of those professors who were out of touch with what is happening in schools and that I would always volunteer in classrooms to be in touch with current practice.

I completed my doctoral studies at Arizona State University where I expanded my understandings of ECE. Throughout my program of study, I refined my thoughts for the culminating component of my program, the dissertation. My dissertation was a continuation of my master's thesis which centered on the teaching characteristics of men in ECE. The premise was that I could identify and disseminate the positive qualities men bring to ECE classrooms. Finding myself immersed in the literature, I became disheartened at the prospect of changing societal beliefs about men in ECE. I asked myself, "Could I design an experiment that would identify an inter-vention of some sort that could change individuals' perceptions of men in ECE?" It was a daunting task that was confounded by many other variables, one being if the general public wanted men in ECE would men choose a low paying career? Following many discussions with Joseph Tobin, my advisor, I decided to pursue a dissertation topic that would broaden my research base which would also make me more marketable. I completed my dissertation titled, "Experiences of Preschool Student Teachers in the New Initial Teacher Certification Program at Arizona State University." After my doctorate work, I found employment in a tenure-track position, it would be hard to know whether one is hired for the quality of research, need, or fit at a certain institution.

Part of my research agenda as a professor still involves getting men involved in the lives of young children. Rather than focusing on attracting men into teaching, I have instead focused on another population of men who have direct access and more influence in the lives of young children, fathers. Through research efforts and service to my community, I work with new and expecting fathers to educate these men about the important role they can play in their child's development. Parenting takes two, but more and more children are growing up without a positive male role model. The optimal time to speak with men about becoming a dad is during pregnancy and the birth process. I have found that once men realize how important their role is in their child's life they will participate.

Being a Male in ECE

One of the reasons I began doctoral work in ECE was the opportunity to recruit more men into teaching ECE. This, as I have discovered, is not an easy task. I did not realize how few men were in ECE when I switched majors and began working at the Child Development Center at Ohio University. It only took moments when entering the preschool that my "maleness" was something special. Being a male in an ECE preparation program and as a male teacher in an ECC center, meant more attention, both positive and negative. In the positive sense, I was praised as a male teacher in ECE. Many families voiced their appreciation that their son or daughter was in my classroom and had the opportunity to be with a positive male role model. Personally, I knew I was engaging in meaningful work and these compliments only bolstered my sense of satisfaction. As a male, I often felt like a favorite teacher; however, I still grapple with the idea that this is solely because of my "maleness."

Encouragement

In my experiences of working with pre-service teachers, I have found over-whelmingly that most have known they wanted to be a teacher since they were in the primary grades. This phenomenon occurs most often with young women who, as a girl in grade school, can completely identify with the school teacher who is almost always a caring, friendly female. Men who come to ECE didn't have this model growing up. To help remedy this occurrence and to allow young boys to see that teaching is a viable option, there are some specific measure that can be implemented. If you are a kindergarten teacher, you can initiate a program whereby fourth grade boys read to the children in your class. Conversely, a high school teacher can initiate a similar program specifically for young men. Whatever the strategy, we must get the message out to boys and young men that being involved in a child's life, as a teacher or father, is expected and typical. Other strategies include actively involve fathers in your program. Most fathers are not going to volunteer but if asked, they will participate in the classroom. When teachers educate mothers and fathers on the importance of father and male involvement, dads will want to be involved and moms will be more likely to volunteer the father's time.

Tips for Working with Parents

Parents have a dubious reputation with many pre-service and in-service teachers. They are often viewed as over-demanding people who make a teacher's job that much more difficult. As a teacher, I was a little intimidated by parents, especially as a beginning teacher. I always thought that what I was doing in the classrooms wasn't living up to their expectations. This was especially true since my philosophy of teaching centered on a play based emergent curriculum which was often incongruent with what parents expected. The main idea to keep in mind when working with parents is that you as the teacher have a degree in ECE. You know (or should now) what you are doing and why you are doing it. The task for the teacher is to explain to parents your rationale, to somehow condense, for example, an entire semester's course on cognitive development into a brief ten minute conversation when a parent who is picking up their child after school; hence, not an easy task, but teaching is not an easy job. In my current position, I emphasize to my students that parents are their allies. Parents know their child the best and are in fact their child's first teacher and should be valued as such. Part of your job as a teacher is to work with families. Often before a teacher can help a child develop to his or her potential, the teacher must work with the parents to help them secure stable housing or the myriad of social services available in our communities.

Personally, I recall a specific parent-teacher conference I had during my initial years as a teacher. I went into the conference thinking that the student being discussed was doing well in the classroom. The parents weren't thinking the same way. They informed me that coming into the school year they were expecting me as a teacher to be a *"Big Mac"* but what they felt like they received was a *"taco."* The air came out of my sails real quick. I was flabbergasted. I listened to them. Their son was an active child, in my opinion a typical preschool boy. They informed me that they wanted me to break his spirit like someone would break a wild horse. I couldn't do this, and I didn't lead them on to think I would. Fast forward to the end of the year conference—these parents were thanking me for my skills as a teacher and for being a role model for their son. I tell this story to the students in my class to illustrate the point that you as the teacher need to be secured in your beliefs and that while you must listen to parents; you cannot meet their every demand.

Concluding Thought

I find it interesting and relevant in the discussion of my path to ECE that my father's occupation is also female dominated and non-traditional. My Dad is a beautician; as a hair dresser, the majority of his clients are women as are almost all of his co-workers. As a child, I saw that his occupation was different from most of the other fathers I knew. In addition to noticing it was different, I also felt embarrassed that my Dad was a hairdresser. I have since come to terms with this and appreciate that my Dad chose a career that wasn't influenced by societal beliefs. I can't help but wonder how this has shaped me as an individual. Did I realize, because of my father's influence, that I could choose a career that wasn't bound by gender restrictions? I would have to say yes and find it interesting that one of my brothers chose to be a librarian, another female dominated profession and another brother cooks for a living, often associated as a female role.

   An individual's experiences help shape who they are and what they believe they can accomplish or explore with regards to their profession. I saw my Dad working alongside women and realized I could also enter ECE, which was female dominated. Every child should have positive experiences with men early in one's life. This will allow children to see the range of human emotion and to see that men have the ability to be nurturing. Too many young children grow up using media's depictions of men as their role model. Men need to show children they can be caring, responsible, and compassionate. Too many young children grow up without a positive male role model. We need more men in ECE. We need more fathers to be involved in their families.

C. SHELDON WOODS

CONCLUSIONS AND SUMMARY

As far back as I can remember, I wanted to be a teacher of some sort. When I was younger, I played teacher with the neighborhood kids and wanted to be an elementary teacher. I was told by many around me, at the time, that teaching was not work for a man. When I was older, I wanted to teach at a medical school. In the end, I became a science educator working with early childhood, elementary, secondary and higher education students. This journey was not without challenges.

My very first job was working with children who were wards of the county. Most had been removed from the custody of their parents for offenses that no child should have to experience. This resulted in children who were very often distrusting of adults and who hid their fears and insecurities in inappropriate behavior. One of the first things I noticed my first day on the job was that I was that I was the only male staff member. I also noticed that I had been assigned to work with the more difficult children. In fact my administrator said to me that it was good to have a male around for some of the more difficult situations. I was not sure what she meant by that, but I would soon find out.

During lunch time the students were being rewarded with a pizza party. Not all students were allowed to attend this party. Those students who were being punished for breaking rules were assigned to eat lunch with me in the cafeteria. I was not really shocked to see that the students who would be eating lunch with me were all male. One of these young fellows, who I will call Tyrone, was very upset about not getting pizza for lunch. He became very belligerent and verbally abusive. I was told by other staff members to keep him calm and not to let him leave the cafeteria as he was threatening to do. He told me that he was going to have pizza and that I was not going to stop him. I requested that he sit down and eat his food. Before I realized what happened, this little boy who was half my height picked up a fork and longed at me. I was able to bring my hand up in a semi defensive move and was stabbed in the hand. I was in utter disbelief and thought to myself that this was not the first day I had envisioned. Ironically, after this initial episode, Tyrone remained with me the rest of the year and we did not have too many future conflicts. I will admit that I had to work very hard not to hold a grudge against him and to remember that he was just a little boy who was in pain and expressed that pain the only way he knew. I will never forget him and I think about him every time I look at the scar on my hand.

Like many of the contributors to this book, I did not take a direct route to working with young children. My own background was working with late elementary, middle and secondary students. I was afraid that my mere size and bulk would scare young children. In fact, it worked to my advantage at times. I ended up working with young children initially not by choice but of necessity. I was asked to teach an early childhood math and science methods course for a colleague who left mid year for medical reasons. This class had a large clinical component in preschool settings. I was terrified but ended up having a blast with the younger students. I was pleased by their natural curiosity and desire to learn and experience new things. Also everything seemed to excite them and impress them. I enjoyed this experience so much so, that later I took a leave from my university faculty position and volunteered to be a computer teacher for early primary grade students at a school on the Westside of Chicago. This was welcomed break. I found myself energized by the younger students.

It was during this period of time that I really saw the impact that a male teacher had on a class of young students. Not taking away from the outstanding jobs done by my female counterparts. Many of who were doing incredible instructional feats with limited resources. I did, however, notice the behavior of the students in my class was not as it was with some of my female counterparts. My female counterparts dealt with behavior problems very swiftly and kept the students in line. But this was very often accomplished with the yelling to get the students attention. They could be heard all over the building.

Early on, I had the usual boundary testing that children try with new teachers. I noticed more of the male students initially exhibited inappropriate behaviors. They were off task, talking of harassing classmates. It was nothing that I saw as inhibiting the learning in the classroom. I did explain the rules several times and did so without yelling or raising my voice. This seemed to be most effective for me and the off task behavior subsided. The biggest challenge I faced that first week came from a female student who was very social and often off task. After repeated attempts to get her to do her work, I moved her to a work station near me. This student, who I will call Keisha, was upset about being moved away from her friends. So, she proceeded to sit and stare at me with a glare that was meant to intimidate me. I initially ignored her and went on with class. When it was clear that Keisha was not going to do her work and that she was intent on trying to stare me down, I locked eyes with her. I was determined that I would not let her intimidate me and that I would not loose this stare down. After what felt like an eternity, she broke into a smile which was followed by a playful laugh. She returned to her work. From that day forward she insisted that she sit next to my work station and I never had problems from her again. In fact, she usually mastered the task at hand quickly and was able to offer assistance to me or to her classmates. My female counterparts remarked at how well the students behaved while they were in the computer lab. When asked how I did it, I was at a loss for words. There was nothing that I could think to say that would not seem trivial or sexist. So I just shrugged my shoulders. I do believe that my gender, size and race played a big part in how the students behaved and learned in my class. I am African-American, 6'2" and 290 pounds.

In my 17 years in the field of education, I have made several observations based on my personal experiences as a classroom teacher and teacher educator:

1. Males who enter education are very often encouraged to teach in secondary or middle school settings.

2. Males who choose to work in early childhood or early elementary often have their masculinity/manhood questioned or worse yet, have their motives questioned.
3. Male teachers are often assigned more students with behavior problems because it is thought they will do a better job with discipline.
4. There are very few male students in elementary education programs and even fewer in early childhood education programs.
5. There are dismally low numbers of males of color in teacher education programs being prepared to work with young students.

It is imperative that male students wishing to work with younger students be encouraged and supported The contributors to this book are from different races, social economic backgrounds; however, they have in common their desire to contribute to the development of students. They would all argue that they have made a difference in the lives of youth they have worked with and it has been reciprocal process.

It bears repeating that this book was by no means meant denigrate the work of female teachers. It is a work that is meant the encourage men to go where they belong and to follow their dreams into classroom or other settings where they may work with young children and students. It is a celebration of the contributions made by male educators who are often out numbered and not respected for their career choices. It is important that students are exposed to both male and female educators so that they can have a balanced image of gender and gender roles.

Implications

The purpose of this book was to bring the practical challenges of being male and an early childhood or early elementary teacher in contemporary society out into the open. To further a dialogue that has not received much attention. The stories that were shared were from practicing teachers who work in a variety of school settings and who are deeply committed to making a difference in the lives of children, their families, and their communities.

As we move forward and encourage men to go into the classrooms youth centers and day care centers where they belong please keep in mind that our world our world and society are changing. We are faced with the challenges of raising children who must deal with the uncertainties of family and life. Hence, the issue of having children exposed to male role models in their developmental years is important (Stroud, Smith, Ealy, & Hurst, 2000). Therefore, the challenge of attracting males into early childhood, elementary education, and other fields that deal with young children is a major hurdle that must be made. Our general society has a phobia against men working directly with young children (Galley, 1992). However; the lack of men in the lives of young children is detrimental to s child's development and identities.

The contributors of this book recommend the following to men seeking to go where they belong:

1. Your influence and the relationships that you build with your students along with an unconditional positive regard them will speak more for your level of work than any test score ever could.
2. Keep the child's best interest in mind and make it your first priority.

3. Teachers and students fates are linked so as students achieve and excel so do teachers.
4. Adequate pay and benefits will help bring a more gender balanced work force o work with your children.
5. Those in power must be willing to share their control and power, and allow men to have a more balance impact on the field.
6. Make sure parents understand that you have an open classroom and that you see them, the parent, as experts on their children.
7. Think through appropriate interaction with children because society does view you with suspicion and questions your competency.

The contributors of this book hope they begin to shatter some of the stereotypes of men in the lives of young children and offer some insight to developing program, policies, and services to recruit, retain, and support men in teaching and encourage men to go where they belong.

REFERENCE

Galley, M., (1992). Male preschool teachers face skepticism but earn acceptance. *Education Week, 19*(20), 1–10.
Stroud, J. C., Smith, L. L., Ealy, L. T, & Hurst, R. (2000). Choosing to teach: Perceptions of male preservice teachers in early childhood and elementary education. *Early child development and care, 163*, 49–60.

GREGORY UBA

PRACTICAL ADVICE AND RESOURCES

A Few Reasons for the Involvement of Men in Early Childhood Education

1. Many children come from homes where they do not have a consistent male role model.
2. Research indicates that men, even more than women, influence gender roles in children.
3. The roles portrayed by men in the media are generally not the most positive example for children.
4. A small percentage, as low as 2%, of early education teachers are men (0–8 years).
5. Many children do not get to see men and women cooperating with each other with their interest in mind on a regular basis.
6. Boys AND girls can learn that boys and men have a nurturing, caring, respectful relationship with children, women, and other men.
7. The percentage of men involved in CAEYC has remained virtually unchanged.
8. 8 is infinity turned sideways. Grant chose the number 88 for his basketball jersey because it represented double infinity. Uncle Greg told him that infinite was a huge number and Grant thought it was way cool.
9. Men *may* interact and communicate differently with young children, giving the program a wide and inclusive range of appropriate adult-child interaction and communication.
10. Men *may* interact and communicate with young children just like their female counterparts, giving children a consistent example of appropriate guidance.
11. The presence of men in an educational setting gives boys the reinforcement that a learning environment is a place in which they belong.
12. The presence of men in a program may lead to greater participation by the male family members of the children that you teach.
13. The presence of men in a program may help model appropriate interaction and communication skills to fathers, uncles, grandfathers etc.
14. The presence of men in a program may lead to the arrival of more men in program.
15. Children want and enjoy the involvement of men in their lives.
16. Many men want to be involved in the lives of young children, but feel that they are not wanted. A program that indicates that they want male involvement can lead to a change in attitudes within the community.
17. Austin's baseball jersey number was 17. He was happy that teacher Greg actually was interested in this fact.
18. Men are trainable. A program which makes a concerted effort to train males to become appropriately involved in young children's lives can lead to a better world for all children.

19. Men *may* have a new and exciting idea or two about curriculum. The rest of you might learn something.
20. Men sometimes actually make "hella" good teachers.

Ways to Recruit and Retain Men in Your Program

1. Look in non-traditional places for potential male staff. Instead of the Child Development Dept of your local college, post job ads in the Sociology, Psychology, or Recreation departments where men more commonly can be found.
2. Visit a local college class where men are enrolled. Speak to the class about the importance of male involvement. Then make sure that the men get an invitation to send you their résumés.
3. When you interview men for entry-level assistant positions, use words that they might then consider as relevant experience such as coaching experience and tutoring.
4. Examine your program's physical environment. Is it male friendly? Are there "guy" magazines in the lobby and break room?
5. Examine your rules. Do they discourage noise, risk, messy activities? Do they discourage active play participation by staff? Do your rules give equal responsibilities to men for equal job titles? Do your rules limit men in ways that are different than the limits for women in regards to such areas as touch, diapering, toilet learning?
6. Examine your curriculum. Do you value block play, science, take-apart, sports activities?
7. Examine your program's culture. Are staff meetings consensus-driven or results driven? Are men asked to clean, fix, move, carry, assemble things? Are they expected to discipline the "bebe" kids?
8. Examine your staff's attitudes. What are the staff's expectations about the competence, roles and power-relationships of men?
9. Prepare the families for men staff by involving male family members, inviting men students for field work assignments, utilizing male college interns, posting images of male caregivers around the program.
10. Support men once hired by finding them mentors, by inviting other experienced men teachers to do staff development, by supporting their professional development, by valuing their input and ideas.

Resources for Male Involvement

- www.menteach.org
- www.naeyc.org (search men's interest forum)
- UCLA child development center, university village, Moises Roman: mroman@ucla.be.edu
- David Hillman Jr., supervisor, The Role Of Men Academy, City of Long Beach: David_Hillman@longbeach.gov
- Gregory Uba, Connections For Children, gregoryu@cfc-ca.org

EDITORS BIOGRAPHICAL INFORMATION

Dr. Lemuel W. Watson

Dr. Lemuel W. Watson is Professor and Former Dean for the College of Education. He also serves at Executive Director of the Center for P–20 Engagement at Northern Illinois University in DeKalb, Illinois. He completed his graduate work at Indiana University in Bloomington, Indiana. His career spans across various divisions in higher education, faculty and administration; he has numerous experiences in all types of institutions to include public and private and two year colleges where he has been a faculty member and a former Dean. His research interests include examining educational organizations and how their structures, practices, leaders, and policies affect learning, development, and outcomes of individuals and communities, especially historically underrepresented groups. In addition, he examines, through critical theory and policy analysis, the impact that socio-political and socio-cultural factors have on educational organizations and their agents, constituents, resources, and operations. Dr. Watson has been a Senor Research Fellow at the C. Houston Center at Clemson University and Research Fellow at the Institute for Southern Studies at University of South Carolina. He is a Fulbright Scholar and has written articles, books, and served as editor for several volumes related to educational leadership and administration, human development, and higher education. He serves on a number of professional boards and is a member of the Board of Visitors for the National Defense University in Washington, DC. He is a Certified Master Coach by the Behavioral Coaching Institute of Sydney, Australia and a Certified Trainer through the Center for Entrepreneurial Resources at Ball State University at Muncie, Indiana. In addition, he is a Certified Systems Engineer by Electronic Data Systems Corporation (EDS) of Plano, Texas. He has recently been awarded the 2010–2011 U.S. Embassy Policy Specialist (EPS) fellowship by the International Research and Exchanges Board of the U.S. Department of State. Dr. Watson also provides professional opportunities through Watson Consulting Services (www.lwatsoncs.com).

Dr. C. Sheldon Woods

Dr. Woods is Associate Professor in the Department of Teaching and Learning in the College of Education at Northern Illinois University. He has also held teaching positions at Kansas State University and DePaul University. He teaches graduate and undergraduate courses in science methods. He also has extensive experiences in working with male teachers. Dr. Woods has special training in cultural diversity, curriculum development, and AIDS education. Dr. Woods completed his undergraduate work at Prairie View A&M University in Biological Sciences, and has a doctorate degree from Kansas State University in Curriculum and Instruction. Dr. Woods identifies evolution education, community service and volunteerism, and technology education as the three foci for his research plan; he links these to teaching and service. In addition, he has been recognized for his extensive contributions to the community with the DePaul University Public Service Award.

CONTRIBUTING AUTHORS

Terry Bussey – Chapter 11

Terry has worked as an Early Childhood Educator for the past 28 years. He holds a B.A. in Religious & Theological studies and is trained as an Early Childhood Educator level 2. He has worked as a front line staff, a supervisor and a director, and has a particular interest in school aged children. He loves photography and is very passionate about documenting the adventures and experiences of children, as well as teaching and presenting these techniques to others. He also feels quite strongly about the importance of reconnecting kids with nature, and providing gender balance in our childcare settings. Terry is a recent recipient of the Manitoba Child Care Association's Early Childhood Educator of the Year award.

Robert M. Capuozzo – Chapter 15

Robert M. Capuozzo is an Assistant Professor of Early Childhood Education at the University of Alaska Anchorage. During his fifteen-year career in early childhood he has worked as a preschool classroom teacher, parent educator, trainer, teacher educator, and researcher. His research interests include father and male involvement in the lives of young children and issues surrounding preservice teacher education.

Daniel Castner – Chapter 7

Daniel Castner is currently a doctoral student at Kent State University, studying curriculum and instruction with a focus on early childhood education. His research interests include studying the social, emotional, and moral aspects of teaching. He is interested in teachers' capacities to serve as curriculum leaders dedicated to democratic education with liberal ideals. Daniel is a kindergarten teacher in the Stow Munroe-Falls City School district in Stow, Ohio.

Jeff Daitsman – Chapter 6

Jeff Daitsman currently teaches 2-year-olds in an inner-city Chicago child care center. He has been a preschool teacher for over three years. In previous years, he worked as a swimming instructor and a camp counselor for about four years. He has an AAS in Child Development and has conducted classroom research on children's expression of gender identity through their dictated and written stories. He feels that it is important for children to see males in nurturing positions in order to counteract the popular stereotypes relating to masculinity.

Robert Gundling – Chapter 10

Dr. Robert Gundling is an Early Childhood Educator with over 30 years of experience working with children, families, and early childhood professionals. His experience includes teaching kindergarten and first grade in a public school system, working as an administrator of a variety of Early Care and Education programs, government positions in Early Childhood Education, and teaching courses at colleges and universities. He has also been involved in advocacy efforts on behalf of young children, testifying at government hearings and activities with professional organizations. He has presented at local, state and national conferences and served as the coordinator of several publications for Early Childhood Professionals.

Darrell C. Huck – Chapter 2

Darrell C. Hucks received his Ph.D. in Education from the department of Teaching and Learning at New York University's Steinhardt School of Culture, Education, and Human Development. He is an assistant professor of elementary education at Keene State College. He has previously taught courses as an adjunct assistant professor in both the graduate and undergraduate teacher education programs at New York University, Teachers College, Columbia University and Brooklyn College (City University of New York). His areas of interests include: the schooling experiences of Black and Latino males; diversity and multicultural education; teacher education; and school reform. Prior to being a doctoral candidate, he was a public school teacher in NYC for six years.

Shaun Johnson – Chapter 3

Shaun Johnson is an assistant professor of elementary education at Towson University in Baltimore, Maryland. He was an elementary teacher in the DC metro area. His research interests include gender and masculinity within education.

Patrick Lewis – Chapter 5

Patrick Lewis is a storyteller-teacher-researcher with a keen interest in story, narrative identity, and storytelling as teaching. He taught as a primary teacher for 18 years before joining the Faculty of Education at the University of Regina. He is Associate Professor of Early Childhood Education working with pre-service and in-service teachers. In addition to the chapter in this collection he also has various articles in journals; is editor of the online journal *in education* (http://www.in education.ca/); recently co-edited the book *Challenges Bequeathed: Taking up the Challenges of Dwayne Huebner*; and authored *How We Think, but not in School: A Storied Approach to Teaching* both published with Sense Publishers.

Scott A. Morrison – Chapter 4

After teaching for eleven years in a small community school in the mountains of western North Carolina, Scott is now a graduate student at the University of North Carolina at Chapel Hill. His research interests include social and philosophical foundations of education, social studies education, ecojustice, and place-based education.

Will Parnell – Chapter 1

Professor Will Parnell is the pedagogical director of the early childhood schools (www.cdfs.pdx.edu) at Portland State University and is an Assistant Professor in education. He also coordinates the master's specialization in early childhood education for the Graduate School of Education's Curriculum and Instruction Department. His specialty areas are making meaning of studio teaching experiences, researching environments, designs, and cultural equity in early education, documenting young children's learning, and facilitating teacher narratives. Will finished his doctorate in education in 2005, and has been researching the experiences and meaning of Reggio-inspired practices, more recently as they relate to action research projects. Will has been in the early education field since 1986 with a wide background of teaching and leadership, ranging from work in places such as lab schools, parent cooperatives, and public school settings. He has consulted, sits on five boards for children's programs and started several schools for young children.

Loui-Vicente Reyes – Chapter 12

Loui-Vicente Reyes has been in the field of early childhood education for thirty-seven years with a career as a teacher of young children, administrator, leader, professor, and scholar. He is an associate professor in the college of education, department of curriculum and instruction, early childhood and bilingual/TESOL education specialty areas at New Mexico State University. Dr. Reyes has an earned Ph.D. in Curriculum and Instruction with specializations in early childhood education and bilingual/TESOL education and has a completed post-doctorate in educational learning technologies. Loui-Vicente research as praxis interest includes areas in critical early childhood and bilingual education, early childhood education professionalization, and Latino educational leadership and policy. Dr. Reyes has co-authored books and has contributed in numerous publications.

Juan Sanchez – Chapter 8

Mr. Sanchez was born and raised on the south side of Chicago. A graduate of Curie Metropolitan High School, he is a proud product of the Chicago Public School system, where he now works as an elementary school teacher. Mr. Sanchez began his teaching career in 2006 after having worked over 10 years in the aviation field. He seeks to be a positive influence over the youth that he now serves in his school, church, and community.

Bruce S. Sheppard – Chapter 14

Bruce S. Sheppard has been in the Early Childhood Education field for 36 years. He began his career in ECE as a Head Start intern in 1974, and has taught in early child hood programs in Minnesota, Washington, and Oregon. He is a frequent presenter on the issue of men in early education at local and national conferences and has written extensively on the subject.

Gregory Uba – Practical Advice and Resources

Gregory Uba, a graduate of the University of California–Riverside, is the director of program services at Delta Sigma Theta Head Start in Los Angeles. He has worked as a preschool and elementary school teacher for 20 years.

Francis Wardle – Chapter 9

As a high school student, Francis Wardle first worked with young children when he volunteered in a Kindergarten class. Since then he has taught at Da Nahazli School in Taos, New Mexico, and PACERS School in Kansas City. He has also been a Head Start volunteer, education manager, community PC member, and director. He was the National Education Director for Children's World Learning Centers, a camp counselor, and a before-and-after school teacher. Currently Dr. Wardle teaches for the University of Phoenix SAS Program and at Red Rocks Community College. He is a founding board member of the Instituto Estrela do Mar, an annual educational conference in Maceio, Brazil, and a board member of Partners of the Americas International. He has published five textbooks on early childhood education, and many book chapters and journal articles. He has four grown children and one grandchild.

George Yamamoto – Chapter 13

Dr. Yamamoto was born in Honolulu, Hawaii. He has a psychology degree from University of Hawaii. He journey working with young children accidentally. He started working with babies as a part time nanny for two newborn twins and found he had a really good temperament for working with infants. It was later suggested by his mother that he should think about working with younger kids, especially babies. He worked with the community college daycare Keiki Hauoli in their infant/toddler room; with PACT Early Head Start; and The Early School in their infant/toddler unit. Currently, he is working with Kamehameha Schools as a Teaching Assistant in the Hi'ilani Program (Parent-child interaction classes).

CPSIA information can be obtained at www.ICGtesting.com
Printed in the USA
LVOW100937080313

323313LV00001B/25/P

9 789460 914041